DECODING MONEY SERENITY™

The Hidden Psychology Behind
Why You Feel Broke, Lonely & Scared
And the System That Fixes It

SerenityDecoded™

DECODING MONEY SERENITY

Published by Yellow Tail Investment Enterprise, LLC
30 N Gould St, Ste R, Sheridan, WY 82801, United States of America
serenitydecoded.com

ISBN: 979-8-9960104-0-0 (Paperback)
ISBN: 979-8-9960104-1-7 (Hardcover)
First published: 2026. Printed in the United States of America.

DECODING MONEY SERENITY™

LEGAL NOTICES

PSYCHOLOGICAL / MEDICAL: This book is a personal development resource. It does not constitute and should not be understood as: medical advice; psychiatric diagnosis; psychotherapy; cognitive behavioral therapy; clinical counselling; or any regulated mental health service. The author is not a licensed therapist, psychologist, or clinical mental health professional. Reading this book does not create any therapeutic, professional, or advisory relationship.

LEGAL: Nothing in this book constitutes legal advice, legal opinion, or legal representation.

EARNINGS AND RESULTS DISCLAIMER

INDIVIDUAL RESULTS VARY. RESULTS ARE NOT TYPICAL. The financial experiences, transformations, and outcomes described or referenced in this book reflect individual experiences of specific people under their specific circumstances. The Publisher makes no guarantee, express or implied, of any specific financial result from reading or applying the content of this book. Financial outcomes depend on your existing financial situation, discipline, effort, consistency, external economic conditions, and individual psychology — all entirely outside the Publisher's knowledge or control. This disclaimer applies to all financial figures, timelines, and transformation stories referenced anywhere in this work.

CRISIS RESOURCES

Financial stress can significantly affect mental health. If engaging with this content causes or worsens distress, please pause and seek support. US: 988 (call or text, 24/7) · UK: 116 123· Canada: 988 · Australia: 13 11 14 · India: 9152987821 · International: findahelpline.com

These Legal Notices are governed by the laws of the State of Wyoming, United States of America. To the extent any provision is unenforceable, all remaining provisions remain in full force. Nothing herein limits any mandatory statutory rights you hold under the consumer protection laws of your country of residence that cannot lawfully be excluded.

Emergency Injunctive Relief. The parties acknowledge that any breach or threatened breach of the intellectual property, confidentiality, or proprietary rights provisions of this Agreement would cause irreparable harm to the Company for which monetary damages would be an inadequate remedy. Accordingly, the Company and its affiliated entities shall be entitled to seek emergency, preliminary, and permanent injunctive relief, without the requirement to post bond or other security, and without prior notice to the breaching party where circumstances require immediate relief, in any court of competent jurisdiction. This right is in addition to, and not in lieu of, all other remedies available to the Company at law or in equity. The breaching party waives any requirement that the Company demonstrate actual damages or post bond as a condition of obtaining such relief.

Attorneys' Fees. In any proceeding to enforce this Agreement or arising from a dispute hereunder, the prevailing party shall be entitled to recover its reasonable attorneys' fees, costs, and expenses from the non-prevailing party. This bilateral prevailing-party provision applies to all levels of proceeding including trial, arbitration where permitted by applicable arbitration rules, and appeal.

Permissions and licensing enquiries: serenitydecoded.com

Serenity Aligned ™

Is the first behavioral App that cracks the code on why you feel broke, lonely, and scared, and helps you fix it.

And then there's **Aarav The Serenity Genie™**, only availble thru the App. Your 24/7 AI personal companion who knows your pattern, remembers every step of your journey, and shows up exactly when you need him.

SerenityDecoded.com

Table of Contents

INTRODUCTION..1

CHAPTER 1: *The Quiet Weight of Money Stress*..........................15

CHAPTER 2: *Why Guilt Makes Money Problems Worse*.............31

CHAPTER 3: *You Didn't Fail the System - the System Changed* .43

CHAPTER 4: *Your "Two Brains"*...57

CHAPTER 5: *Scarcity Changes the Way You Think*.....................69

CHAPTER 6: *Your Financial Style*..83

CHAPTER 7: *Patterns, Not Willpower*...99

CHAPTER 8: *Emotional Spending isn't Stupidity*.......................113

CHAPTER 9: *Why Most Advice Starts too Late*..........................127

CHAPTER 10: *Building Breathing Room Where There is None*139

CHAPTER 11: *A New Definition of "Enough"*.............................153

CHAPTER 12: *Inflation is a Fact of Life*.......................................165

CHAPTER 13: *Designing a System That Fits Your Life*.............177

CHAPTER 14: *Debt Without the Guilt* 189

CHAPTER 15: *Investing When You're Starting Late…* 201

CHAPTER 16: *Burning Through the Gig Economy* 213

CHAPTER 17: *Measuring Progress Without Obsession* 225

CHAPTER 18: *Money and Life Satisfaction* 237

CHAPTER 19: *Financial Peace is Quieter Than You Think* 249

Dedication

This book is dedicated to the millions of people worldwide seeking financial security and peace. May you be enveloped in the serenity and may money truly help you live the life you deserve.

Introduction

> *If you've ever been scared –from a movie or thrill ride or a car accident, house fire, or anything else, you know it's not a way you want to live every day.*

— — —

Always on edge.

When you're struggling with your finances, when you have money problems, you'll feel like you're on the edge of disaster constantly.

That level of living slows your mental processes. That's the kind of stress that keeps you up at night. The kind that doesn't let your mind rest.

There's no serenity.

You're dealing with *constant* stress. Even if you can't figure out *why* there's stress in your life, even if you don't know exactly what's got you up at night worried, it's stress.

The human brain interprets all stress -regardless of the origin or reason- as a **threat**.

So, your reactions to it are instinctual. It's about survival. It doesn't matter whether you're facing a genuine life-threatening circumstance or can't cover your bills this month: your brain doesn't differentiate.

People who don't struggle financially can't understand those of us who do, especially when you earn a decent salary. They can't understand the constant, everyday strain we experience. They might not understand why we ignore the bills, spend money on things when we're already running out of funds, or can't manage our funds.

Want to know a secret, though? Those people aren't perfect. They may not worry about money, but they're dealing with other types of stress,

even if they haven't yet figured out what that is.

Yes, there are an abundance of financial gurus out there who write books, build courses, have podcasts and call-in shows, websites, and every trick in the book who pound us with guilt for our mistakes, who ask, "Why did you *do* that?" when we confess our sins.

Do we need to listen to them? Not always. Sure, their advice is often sound and they certainly know what they're talking about as far as budgeting and investing and so forth is concerned, but like the diet fads and exercise masters of the world… if they were actually helping people -not just short-term, but long-term help- then obesity and a lack of physical fitness wouldn't be a *growing* problem in some parts of the world.

Just as financial stress wouldn't be a continually growing and increasing problem globally[1].

1 Eric Johnson. The 'vibecession' has gone global, with citizens around the world fearing an unsustainable financial future. Apr. 3, 2024. https://www.cnbc.com/2024/04/03/the-vibecession-has-goneglobal.html#:~:text=Rising%20prices%20and%20pessimism%20about,%25)%20and%20Singapore%20(46%25).

But it is.

Why?

Because all the traditional tools, models, guides, and scolding don't help change behavior. Before you change behavior, you must first *understand* it. You need to understand *why* you do the things you do. And before you get to that point, you need to realize and accept that **it's not your fault**.

That's right. This book is about helping *you*, not blaming you. Helping you, not shaming you. Helping you, not smacking you around and criticizing you.

Because you're human. What you've done and what you're doing is... (brace for it)... ***natural***.

That's right. There's nothing you're doing or have done that isn't a **natural reaction** to the stress in your life.

So, first things first: we're going to tear down the walls you've built around you and this problem. We're going to rid the negative feelings about money from your life. We're going to strip away all this guilt and feelings of inferiority about your finances.

Then we'll be able to make *lasting* change.

THE MYTH OF THE 'NORMAL' FINANCIAL LIFE

Social media is quite a monster. Sure, many of us think it's cool, a great way to 'stay connected' to family or friends, or a means to find validation.

It *can* be those things, but it can also be a vampire. It can suck truth out of your life. It can even alter the way you view the world around you.

One of the biggest issues with social media (in my view) is that it **amplifies** *only* the things people *want* everyone else to see (about them).

It's a way to create a false version of you where everything is great, your marriage is awesome, your house is immaculate, your job is the best, or your kids are angels.

But it's not true. Hey, I'm not saying people are lying, but they're definitely not sharing everything.

People don't go on social media and say, "I lost my temper today and cursed out my boss," or, "I cut someone off in traffic and didn't care," or, "My wife and I had our third screaming match of the week already."

Social media allows us to portray the life we want other people to see, even when it's *far* from reality.

Life is a battle. It's ugly at times. So are relationships, work, and every aspect of our days. But we tend to hide the ugliness and the dark times from the world around us.

We do this because we *think* our life is way worse than it is and we just want to *feel* good about *something*. When we feel good about something, our body produces a hormone in the brain called dopamine.

Dopamine is a neurotransmitter that's often labeled the 'feel good' hormone. The 'happy hormone[2].' It's a chemical messenger between nerve cells, and it connects to the rest of your body.

It plays a small role in our survival instinct. While I'm not going to get into *why* or *how* it helps in that response (because we'd be talking about vasodilation and more, which'll put you to sleep), it can and often does provide a sense of pleasure. This increases motivation to keep doing (or do again) the things that helped us feel good (that created the increased production in dopamine).

2 How to Boost Feel-Good Hormones Naturally (Henry Ford Health). May 3, 2021. http://henryfordhealth.com/blog/2021/05/how-to-boost-feel-good-hormones-naturally

When you have people clapping for you, patting you on the back, or praising you for your social media posts, your brain produces a shot of dopamine[3].

It *feels* good!

There's a **reward** in sharing *only* the positive aspects of life, the things people will praise you for.

But what happens when you start looking around at all those "amazing" lives everyone else seems to be living (because they're after that same feel-good emotion)? You begin comparing your life to theirs, and it never seems to measure up.

I don't know that there's any other subject where this plays such a role as in our financial life.

You see people posting pictures about their awesome family. You see a friend remodeling their house (the before and after pictures are to die for!). Someone's child just got accepted to a prestigious university. Or they gained a promotion!

Before long, we start thinking:

- *They're doing so much better.*
- *They seem so much more stable than I.*
- *They've got it all together... and then some.*

This doesn't mean you're jealous. It means you doubt. You feel you're behind on things you can't quantify. Then you start to wonder why no one else is struggling like you are, and subsequently the stress you feel must be your fault.

3 Dopamine. Cleveland Clinic. March 23, 2022. https://my.clevelandclinic.org/health/articles/22581-dopamine

This is all rooted in the myth of the "normal" financial life[4]. This myth is extremely dangerous. It can also be one of the most damaging tales we tell ourselves; that everyone else has got it together.

THE SILENT MAJORITY

I want to tell you a secret. Okay, it's not so much a 'secret' as merely something people don't know much about.

Whatever your financial situation, regardless of the mistakes or decisions or pain and stress you're dealing with right now, many people feel uncertain about their finances, too.

Most people don't talk about it. They may appear confident in their status and position financially, even if they *feel* unsettled or uneasy.

What you don't see is how they're juggling obligations, making compromises, managing stress, and even doing the same kinds of constant calculations silently that you do.

Most people tend to remain silent about their financial struggles or stresses. This creates the illusion that they're 'just fine.'

The moment people realize that money is a marker of success, responsibility, or even 'adulthood,' they learn quickly what to share and what to hide. Struggle, stress, doubt, or fear about money becomes something to hide and stability becomes something to 'perform.'

This is how the myth perpetuates and grows bigger with time.

4 Dr. Charles Chaffin. Comparison is the Thief of Joy … and sometimes, Financial Well-being (LinkedIn Pulse). Sept. 15, 2024. https://www.linkedin.com/pulse/comparison-thief-joyand-sometimes-financial-wellbeing-chaffin-pyo5e#:~:text=Comparison%20doesn't%20just%20encourage,are%20perpetually%20enjoying%20sunny%20skies?

A MORE HONEST WAY TO LOOK AT PROGRESS

I want you to stop looking at everyone else and instead focus on you.

You are unique. Your life is unique. Your experiences are unique. The path you took that has led you here is unique.

Stop acting as though you're on the same road as those around you or family members or friends or coworkers.

Let it go.

Instead of trying to determine what's 'normal' as a financial situation, I want you to look at your own financial choices.

Do your financial choices make sense given your *actual* life? Does it? Based on:

- Your income.
- Your responsibilities.
- Your health.
- Your history.
- Your upbringing.
- Your margin (or lack of one).

Progress isn't the same between one person and the next, nor should we expect it to be. Gaining stability over time under pressure doesn't have less value than stability gained quickly with little to no pressure. It just means you had to work harder for it.

There's nothing wrong with that. There's also nothing wrong with making a bunch of mistakes along the way to get there.

Stripping away the imaginary benchmark or standard you've compared yourself to allows you to focus on self-assessment that's based on reality, not illusion.

That's a great starting point.

MOVING FORWARD WITHOUT THE WEIGHT OF COMPARISON

In order to develop lasting change, we need to first set aside self-judgment. You are unique. You are special. No other person on this planet has lived or is living *your* life.

We need to let go of guilt, excuses, inaccurate expectations, and even comparison traps.

We want to reach a place where our finances are manageable on the inside, not impressive to the outside. You deserve financial calm, even when the storms erupt around you.

When you're constantly chasing 'normal,' you're expending too much energy. You're living a *real* life and that means dealing with real problems, not someone else's made-up facades.

STRESS 'BLEEDS'

Stress can (and often does) affect every area of life. You feel it at night when your body is exhausted, your brain doesn't want to function properly, but the thoughts won't stop flowing.

You feel it on the way to work, while you're pouring yourself out on the job doing the best you can, and still on your way home.

You feel it when you get paid, knowing practically that entire paycheck is already going to somewhere and someone else.

You get through the days. You cope the best you can. Nothing's on fire (yet). You don't have a raging inferno blasting through your life, family, or work.

At the same time, nothing feels safe. It's as though there's a monster in your home, but you can't see or hear it or touch it, but you *feel* it.

It's as though you're bleeding slowly and it just won't stop. At some point you worry about what happens if you can't stop the blood flow. For a living body, eventually the heart will stop.

Prolonged, unrelenting stress can sometimes cause the same effect in us.

It's easy to assume that financial stress looks like chaos. Missed mortgage or rent payments, collection calls, an inch or two away from losing everything, but for the majority of us, that's not the case.

For us, the bills are (mostly) paid. Our credit cards are (mostly) not maxed out. We make regular payments. Life is (mostly) moving forward relatively fine.

From the outside, everything looks okay.

But inside, the heaviness presses down.

YOU'RE NOT ALONE

It's easy to think you're alone in this, that none of your friends, family, neighbors, or coworkers are dealing with this kind of stress.

It's easy to think that, but it's not true. Hundreds of millions of people lack serenity with their finances.

In fact, you may not even know *why* you struggle to sleep at night, why you constantly feel 'on edge,' as though some disaster is about to strike. You may be one of those middle-income people who keep up with your bills, pay them off every month on time (even early), and still feel pressure closing in.

You want to know the ironic thing about stress? When we can't pinpoint the precise reason for the stress, human nature seeks **relief** from it, but it's almost as though there's no way to decode the secrets to serenity.

That often comes in the form of what psychologists refer to as maladaptive behaviors[5], or short-term decisions. This could include substance abuse, buying things you don't need or can't afford, or putting tasks off.

I want to stress a very important point here: **this doesn't mean you're irresponsible.**

This is critical.

Yes, you could make bad decisions. Yes, you might put off paying a few bills. Yes, you may spend money you know you shouldn't (to buy something you don't need), simply because it *feels* good at that time.

That still doesn't make you irresponsible.

It makes you human.

WHAT THIS BOOK IS –AND ISN'T

This book is a journey. It's a journey from where you *are* to where you *will be.*

This book is a guide. It's a mentor who walks beside you, understands you, and listens to you. Yeah, I know a 'book' doesn't listen, but there's more to a book than words on a page.

This book is a gateway. It's part of a larger community, a community of people just like you and me who have dealt with these same challenges you've believed are only yours.

This book is a mirror. It's easy to look down on yourself, get down on yourself, and feel defeated, but when you see yourself in a mirror, you'll

5 Why We Procrastinate: The Psychology of Putting Things Off. July 13, 2025. Deconstructing Stigma.https://deconstructingstigma.org/guides/procrastination#:~:text=So%20Why%20Do%20We%20Procrastinate,Perfectionism.

see a person who deserves a chance, a person who tries, a person who *will*…

This book isn't a hammer. I have no desire to smack anyone over the head for things they've done in the past.

This book isn't a guilt meter. There's no feeling bad here, and if you feel bad, I'm giving you permission to not just let that go but throw it far away from you. There's no room for guilt here. We're all human. We're all flawed. It's okay. And I'm going to help you throw that all away.

This book isn't going to tell you to 'try harder' or pretend you've got extra money lying around or trick you with fancy tools and sleights of hand to effectively use a Band-Aid over a deep wound.

No, this book is about bringing serenity into your life.

This book is about helping you understand what's happening -inside your head, inside your habits, inside the modern financial landscape (that you have no control over)- so you can move forward without carrying all this extra invisible weight.

This book is about closing the hatch *before* the storms hit.

- This isn't about **urgency**.
- This isn't about **fear**.
- This is about **clarity**.

ONE LAST WORD: WHO AM 'I'?

This book is written in the first-person, but there's no typical 'I' involved here. It is not AI-written. This was crafted by a real human.

Don't spend time and energy trying to figure out who 'I' am. Instead, recognize that this book was the product of people just like you who have 'been there, done that' and struggled through a wealth of information, tools, tips, strategies, and resources before anything lasting stuck.

'I' was honored to be able to write this… for *you*.

You're what matters.

Personal Steps

In each chapter of this book (you will come to 'Personal Step' sections.

These Personal Steps are designed for *you*. Please read and complete them. When you do, and use the Serenity Aligned™ app (see back of book) to answer the questions or fill in the information from these steps, you'll be helping your virtual mentor, **Aarav The Serenity Genie™** to learn more about you and help support you along this journey.

You don't need to share your answers or information with anyone. It's *only* for you.

Can you skip them? Sure. It's your book. You can do what you want with it, but I assure you… if you do them, you'll be much further along by the end than if you don't, and the level of support and encouragement and guidance you'll receive from Serenity Aligned™ (see back of book) and Aarav The Serenity Genie™ will be so much stronger.

This book was designed to go along with our Serenity Aligned™ app (see back of book), a companion, a guide, a behavioral support and mentor. Together, it's life-changing.

You'll have questions. At times you'll feel a little lost, unsure what to do or if what you're thinking or feeling is okay. There will be moments when you *know* what to do, but just can't make yourself do it.

Aarav The Serenity Genie™ is there for you. So will a growing community of others, just like you, who have gone and are going through the same challenges, doubts, and struggles you are and will be, and who are also using Serenity Aligned™ (see back of book) and staying connected through our community.

Can you do this alone? Sure, but the road will be much tougher. A cord of three strands is not easily broken. Help in difficult times always makes us stronger.

Alright, now, without further ado, let's get started on the path to your new future...

Part One

You Are Not Bad With Money

CHAPTER 1

The Quiet Weight of Money Stress

You're not bad with money ... you're under pressure.

— — —

THE DARKNESS ENVELOPES YOU. PERHAPS SOMEONE IS LYING NEXT TO you, deep asleep. You wish you could be there, too, in dreamland, but your mind won't stop running through a flood of thoughts. You're not panicking. But you're not at peace, either.

You may be thinking about your next paycheck. It might be the same as the last one and the one before that, but it already feels gone. The bills keep coming. Like a dull headache that won't leave you alone, it's right there, tapping at the edge of your skull. 'Remember me?' It says. 'I haven't left you yet.'

You're tired. No, you're beyond tired. You're worn out worrying about everything, but what can you do? There are only so many hours in the day.

You've opened your banking app a dozen times this week, checking the dwindling balances. There's *something* in your savings account, which is good, but it's not much. But your checking account, now that's another story.

For years you've worked hard to bring the numbers up, and for a while you did well. You read a book, reworked your numbers, and even started paying down your debts (beyond the minimums), but prices rose faster than you had anticipated, and here you are, again, staring into the dark unable to sleep. Serenity still feels a lifetime away. Contentment and peace like a distant relative you'll never see.

There are millions of people throughout the world who have done nearly everything 'right' with and about money, who earn a decent wage, but still find themselves stressed, struggling to sleep, and worried about the future.

Some of us get bills in the mail and shove them aside, unopened, where they will wait (im)patiently for some 'later time.' And they never go quietly. Not for long. Even if you successfully manage to ignore a stack of bills, reminders keep slipping in through the mail, through your email, and now even to your phone via text messages.

There are some who have gone shopping for food for the week, only to stand in the checkout line looking over their careful selections and wonder if they have enough to cover this purchase.

No matter the level of stress you feel because of your finances, it's stress and stress seeps into everything.

STRESS 'LEAKS'

Back in 2015, there was a 790-foot cargo ship called the SS El Faro that took off from Jacksonville, Florida in the U.S. bound for San Juan, Puerto Rico. Through a series of bad decisions, it sailed into Hurricane Joaquin.

A small hatch door had been left open on deck. Normally, this would pose little to no danger, but with swelling seas and waves smashing against the hull of the ship and pounding up onto the deck, water poured into the hatch and down into the cargo holds. Eventually, the ship lost propulsion and as more water seeped in through that small hatch door, it began to lean until it finally capsized, killing all 33 crew members on board[6].

Small openings are no big deal when the weather's fine, but when the storms hit, they can destroy everything.

It's the same with stress in your life. And just like with water in a cargo ship, stress can weigh you down, pull on you, drag you off balance, and eventually cause you to collapse.

In many cases, financial stress doesn't come from one **big** problem, but rather a hundred smaller ones that don't ever get resolved. It shows up as:

- Rechecking numbers you already know,
- Delaying decisions, not because you don't care, but because you care too much,
- Guilt after buying something you can technically afford,
- The constant sense that you're just one wrong move away from everything unraveling.

---

6 Susan Miller. Captain's Mistakes Led to El Faro Sinking, Coast Guard Report Says (USA Today). Oct. 1, 2017. https://www.usatoday.com/story/news/2017/10/01/captains-mistakes-led-el-faro-sinking-coast-guard-report-says/721037001/#:~:text=Capt.,save%20it%2C%20the%20report%20added.

It's the background calculations that keep running in your head all day long, like:

- *If I do this, what's going to happen later?*
- *If something goes wrong, will I be able to afford it?*
- *Am I not doing something I should be doing?*

You don't feel settled and it's exhausting.

Stress, over time, leaks into anxiety. Give anxiety enough free time and reign in your life and you end up dealing with a whole host of *other* challenges and problems to deal with. Physical health problems arise. Relationship struggles ensue. And so on.

This is the 'stress leak.' It's confusing, too, because even though you're stressed, you're functioning. You show up to work on time, every day. You pay what you can. You're making an effort.

Yet it's like you're **bracing** for something… all the time.

Imagine you're walking down the street and suddenly a car screams your way, weaving around, tires screeching. Your focus becomes fine-tuned to that **one thing** in front of you that's a perceived threat.

It doesn't matter if that car will ever leave the road and jump onto the sidewalk or directly into your path. It could regain control and just be a reckless driver with a heavy foot.

What matters is how ***you*** *perceive* the threat. Or, more accurately, how your ***brain*** perceives it. You tense up. Your brain is preparing your body to stand its ground or flee (run).

That's the way it is with regular stress in life. Your brain doesn't recognize that there's no *immediate* threat. It's only taking the information your experiences are providing for it and reacting.

When you're operating on a very thin margin for error -be it financial, physical, mental, or even emotional- it can feel like you're failing.

But you're not.

When there's not much room for error, your nervous system notices.

Inflation spikes, the slow cost-of-living increases, stagnant wages, a new baby, divorce, an aging parent or grandparent needing more care and support, or any number of external factors can cause those margins you had to shrink. Even if you don't consciously label it a threat, your brain does.

And like that car racing down the road that grabs your full attention, if that happens every time you go anywhere –to work, the store, to pick up the kids, etc.— it will wear you down.

Your brain stays alert[7]. The amygdala is the part of the brain that focuses on survival. It's constantly scanning for danger.

It's not because you're dramatic. It's because your brain is adaptive, instinctual about survival, always scanning, always seeking danger to protect your life.

You're carrying a *lot* without much cushion. All that stress leaks into everything else.

Money stress doesn't often stay contained in one narrow aspect of life. It leaks. It spreads into the cargo holds of other areas.

It leaks into **sleep**. You keep treading the same ground and thoughts you've always stomped over countless times.

It leaks into **relationships**. Conversations become tense. Talking about the bills or income or anything else eventually stops, adding to the strain.

7 Saya Des Marais. Hypervigilance: Why you feel stuck in 'fight or flight' (Rula). Sept. 5, 2025. https://www.rula.com/blog/hypervigilance/

It leaks into **decision-making**. The once 'small,' insignificant decisions suddenly feel heavier than they used to, or should.

It leaks into your self-perception. You begin thinking everyone else is doing fine, that somehow you missed the class on managing your finances. You believe you should be further along now than you are, that you should be 'better' than this. You begin questioning your judgment, your choices, yourself.

FIGHT OR FLIGHT

Tens of thousands of years ago, humans lived in wild, rugged places. Most were tribal communities in tents or living in caves or crude mud and mortar structures. They hunted and gathered for their daily survival.

And they were hunted as well.

Tigers, lions, crocodiles in the water, sharks, mountain lions or pumas or cougars, wolves, bears, and more were all capable of hunting humans down.

Just like animals, we're equipped with a base survival mechanism crudely labeled 'fight or flight' responses.

Whenever the nervous system (your senses, brain, etc.) detects a potential threat (you might hear rustling in the leaves, a growl, or see a wild animal charging you), your body reacts.

It might pique your senses, allowing you to focus on sounds or smells or sights more keenly. It might ramp up the production of adrenaline or other chemicals and hormones in the body.

The brain and nervous system are preparing the body to either stand firm (fight) or run like they've never run before to escape (flight).

Now, most of us in modern times don't face those kinds of threats much (or at all). Sure, there are regions torn apart by war, under constant threat of bombs or guns or assaults, but most people in the world live in more urban, civilized areas where threats of that nature are few and far between.

This human survival instinct may be dulled for most, but it's still there and still quite ready to take action.

However, your brain doesn't differentiate between a real, immediate physical threat and a perceived emotional or financial one. "It's not just external threats that trigger the amygdala. Negative self-talk such as thoughts like "I'm failing," "I can't handle this," or "I'm not good enough," can activate the same stress circuits as real-world dangers[8]."

Stress is the reaction to stimuli. Stress is the prepared mode for fighting or fleeing.

When we're feeling financial pressure and it is regular or constant, your brain will seek relief.

It will find escape however it can, even through delaying dealing with the issue or simply buying something that makes you happy (because that gives you a hit of dopamine, a hormone in the brain associated with feeling good).

Yes, you need to take responsibility for your choices and actions, but what you've been dealing with and what you've been doing to navigate the money pressure in your life doesn't prove you're irresponsible.

It only proves you're human, and you're surviving.

8 Your Brain's Job Is to Keep You Alive – Not Necessarily to Keep You Calm (Health Psychology Partners). https://www.healthpsychologypartners.com/articles/your-brains-job-is-to-keep-you-alive#:~:text=The%20Brain%20Doesn't%20Know,a%20chance%20to%20weigh%20in.

YOU'RE NOT WEAK

You're not. You're actually strong. You may not believe that now, but as we move through this book, you'll begin to understand.

If you were weak, you wouldn't be reading this. If you were weak, you'd have given up. If you were weak, you'd just continue going the way you've been going.

You're not weak. You're strong. Even though it *feels* like weakness, that feeling happens because stress reduces your **bandwidth**. When money requires your constant attention, it competes with everything else going on in your life, and everything else that (also) needs attention.

The ultimate cost of stress and its seeping into every other aspect of life isn't financial.

It's mental. It's emotional. It's in your relationships.
And yes, *that* can have a financial cost you don't anticipate, too.
Most people carry all this weight silently.

It's time to change that. While you consume this book, engage with the Serenity Aligned™ app (see back of book), talk to **Aarav The Serenity Genie™**, and you will come to a place free of judgment, of lasting financial calm.

THE HIGHEST REEL PROBLEM

We opened the intro talking about social media and its impact on how we view ourselves. With the way social media infects every aspect of life these days, what we tend to see of other peoples' lives is called the 'highest reel[9].'

9 Rojan Baby. The Impact of Instagram Reels on Mental Well-being and Productivity (Medium). Oct. 1, 2023. https://medium.com/@rojanbaby123/the-impact-of-instagram-reels-on-mental-well-being-and-productivity-ac8c40cb99f2

A reel refers to a movie reel. When shooting a movie or TV show, directors call for many takes, then they sit in an editing booth and sift through them all for the best.

The finished product is basically the highest reel: the best footage.

That's what we get with social media; the **best** results.

People don't usually share their stress and anxiety; they share the outcome when everything works out right. They don't talk about downturns and tradeoffs; they talk about the results. They don't post about their struggles; they post about the moment it all paid off.

You (and we) see the highest reel, the best footage of others' lives.

Let's look at a few other examples just to make sure we're all understanding this concept.

Someone might talk about a promotion, but not the ups and downs leading to it, or the times they were passed over or almost lost their job.

You may see the beautiful home a friend just bought, but not the debt they now carry or how they, too, are basically living paycheck to paycheck.

When you compare your life's full experiences -the good and the bad- to someone else's polished, highest reel footage, it's not a fair comparison.

Not even close.

Reality always loses out in that scenario. And so does any (real) chance at attaining financial serenity.

PERSONAL ACTION STEP 1: EXPECTATIONS

As we step into these Personal Steps, let's start with expectations. In order to know where we're going, we need an idea of where we're starting.

Open the Serenity Aligned™ app (see back of book) and write down three financial expectations you have taken on for yourself over time for this step (you may also answer these Personal Steps in this book, but when you work within the app, Aarav The Serenity Genie™ will be able to offer more personalized, structured support.

Some of your expectations could be things like:

"By now, I should have..."

"People my age are usually..."

"If I was doing this right, I'd have..."

Expectation 1: ______________________________

____

____

____

Expectation 2: ______________________________

____

____

____

Expectation 3: ______________________________

____

____

____

Next to each one you've listed, answer: *where did this expectation come from?*

Take time and do your best to try and figure out (or remember) where this expectation arose from. Was it from a parent? A friend? A book you read?

Once you've figured that out and written it down, consider this: *Does it fit my life now?*

A lot of expectations we have as younger people don't fit our life when we age, when we have a family, when we change.

Serenity Aligned™ (see back of book) will save your answers if you do them there, and that will allow you to see just how far you're coming along with your progress as you move closer to lasting peace and serenity!

These answers don't need to be perfect. They should be honest, though. Outgrowing expectations isn't failure. It's another form of adaptation, and that's a significant part of survival.

THE RESPONSIBILITY SHIFT

You've made mistakes, yes. You've made some decisions you wish you could undo. You've gone down a path you never intended to traverse, and it might feel like there's no way back.

Ultimately, *only* you can right the ship and get to where you want to be. I can't do it for you. Your spouse or partner or best friend can't wave a magic wand and change everything in your life.

You may feel you've been 'irresponsible' for years, but I'm telling you to let that go. Yes, you must take responsibility, but we also need to lay the initial groundwork for what comes next: removing the constant feelings of guilt.

If your financial situation and especially your decisions and actions have caused irreparable harm to others or to relationships, there's nothing you can do about that. Not now.

In time, you can address that. In time, you'll be able to heal, just as those who may be hurt will heal.

We are pliable beings; we can change and we can grow and learn and become better.

So, while I want you to understand your past doesn't mean you were or are irresponsible, you do need to take responsibility. That's the only way any of this will work.

BE AWARE OF YOUR LANGUAGE

I'm not sitting here telling you to stop cursing or being crude and obnoxious (if that's who you are). I'm telling you to beware of the language you use to **describe** *you*.

When finances get tough, people tend to search for some moral explanation. That often comes out as, *"I'm just not good with money."*

Or, *"I don't have enough discipline, so it's all my fault."*

Or, *"I should know better."*

Or, *"What's wrong with me?"*

That doesn't help anyone, least of all you, so I need you to stop if you've ever done that, especially recently.

Those statements are desperate attempts to explain the flooding in the cargo holds of your life. It won't close the hatch. It won't stop the leak.

It will only keep you burying your head in the sand, avoiding any real potential solutions.

What you *can* say are things like:

- **I'm under pressure.**
- **I'm managing competing needs and doing the best I can.**
- **I'm making decisions in a situation that doesn't offer much wiggle room.**

It doesn't mean that every choice you made in the past was the best one possible; it simply means you were trying to navigate real constraints.

Yes, we need to take responsibility for our choices, but the days of self-punishment or feeling constant guilt over them **is <u>over</u>**.

Done.
Finished.

Aarav The Serenity Genie™ is a powerful resource that can help remind you of this, if you let it. It celebrates the days you show up, not the times you fall short.

PERSONAL ACTION STEP 2: REFLECTION

Open Serenity Aligned™ (see back of book) and take some time to think about the past week or two in your life. Then write down *three times* from

these past couple weeks when money stress showed up.

None of these instances have to be dramatic. They could have been fleeting, but if you remember them, that's important.

They could have been:

- A moment of hesitation involving an expense.
- A knot in your stomach.
- A decision you delayed for financial reasons.
- A thought that kept on playing over and over.

For each moment, write down:

- What was happening (ie. Where were you? What were you doing? Etc.)
- What you felt (physically and/or emotionally).
- What you avoided or postponed or overthought.

That's it.

You're not solving anything yet. You're not grading yourself. You're merely learning how stress **speaks** in your life.

This is about **awareness**. And *that's* about preparedness.

Aarav The Serenity Genie™ will Personalize your journey so when you ask questions, have doubts about a decision, or need extra guidance through this journey financial calm, it will strengthen your path.

ONE LAST WORD OF ENCOURAGEMENT

Rome wasn't built in a day. Yes, I know that's cliché, but some of the best statements are used often.

You don't need to have your finances figured out before you can feel okay. Your world isn't falling apart today. Or tomorrow.

Making changes isn't about making it perfect. It's about **progress, not perfection**.

And it's okay to feel fear. You can still move forward. That's what true courage is, actually. Courage isn't the absence of fear; it's experiencing fear and still pressing on.

If money and finances feel heavy, it's not because you're broken or bad or wrong. It's just that you've been carrying too much weight.

In the chapters ahead, we're going to talk about *why* this stress takes the shape it does in your life and what actually helps when life doesn't offer neat margins or lines (that you can color inside of).

For now, it's enough to know that…

- **You're not behind.**
- **You're not failing.**
- **And you're not alone.**

That's right. There's a growing community of people **just like you** who are here to support you in this journey. All you've got to do is connect and stay connected to it. That's one of the core reasons we built The Serenity Aligned™ app (see back of book)… to be *your* support and guide along this path to serenity.

Together, we can!

CHAPTER 2

Why Guilt Makes Money Problems Worse

Feeling guilt over your finances isn't truth. It's the story you were handed.

— — —

YOU'VE PROBABLY ASSUMED THAT AVOIDING YOUR FINANCES IN THE past was because you don't care. (Okay, perhaps you haven't 'avoided' them, but at some point you've questioned yourself or delayed paying a bill or put off running to the store for something you needed.)

That's wrong thinking. It was because you *did* (and do) care.

You have a natural survival instinct *and* mechanism in you. It's hard-wired into your very being. We all possess this survival tool.

It runs millions of calculations a second, determining whether you should stand your ground (fight) or run away (flight).

Now, the human brain is the most advanced organ in history[10]. However, it does have a limitation: it doesn't differentiate between *real* and *imagined* threats. That's why you can wake up from a nightmare in a cold sweat, struggle to gather your bearings, and feel your heart pounding in your chest.

You were asleep! You were *resting*! But your brain perceived a very real threat, even if it was all in your mind.

That's how everyday stress can affect the brain, too. Money stress (or *any* stress, for that matter) is doing the same thing to you. *All the time.* So, when I say that avoiding certain things (like a bill or two) doesn't mean you don't care, that it means you care too much, what I'm saying is you're in a type of 'survival mode.'

<u>You're trying to protect yourself</u>. Subconsciously, to varying degrees.

It's not that you're apathetic to your bills or creditors or thin bank account; it's that there's discomfort surrounding it and that leads to stress, and that often leads to guilt.

Guilt has a nasty habit of turning attention into a threat.

When you feel guilty over something you've done or are avoiding, guess what? *Any* attention you give to that 'thing' adds to the threat level. In your brain. In those millions of calculations your mind is running through.

And the moment your nervous system is under threat, it seeks a way to escape.

To avoid.

You're avoidance behaviors are simply about survival and Serenity Aligned™ (see back of book) was built to help you not only recognize

10 Di Loreto & Hurlbert. Human Characteristics: Brains (Smithsonian Institute). http://humanorigins.si.edu/human-characteristics/brains

these behaviors, but to offer gentle encouragement and reminders to support you along this road to financial freedom.

THE AVOIDANCE LOOP NO ONE TALKS ABOUT

Mary was a 36-year-old single mother of two boys. Since her divorce five years ago, she has struggled. For a long time, she was emotionally wounded, trying to navigate life as a single parent following 10 years of a difficult, draining marriage. Eventually her finances suffered.

The court system favored for her ex-husband, and that meant a paltry alimony and meager child support. Mary had been the only one working for two years by the time things fell apart. Her ex had effectively given up looking for work after he lost his job.

That put tremendous strain on their relationship, which eventually caused it to crack and crumble. When Mary looked back, it seemed like *that* strain was pale in comparison to what she was dealing with now.

She wasn't prepared for inflation to rise so fast. Mary was getting by before the pandemic, then suddenly lost her financial footing. The few hundred extra dollars she had in her account quickly became a few measly bucks or pennies after each paycheck.

As time marched on and winter hit, with electricity rate increases and the cost of heating oil, debt built faster than she could keep up with.

Mary would never say she was ashamed of her situation. Yet, there *was* a sense of guilt that made itself known. And that's what we need to realize.

'Guilt' doesn't come announcing itself with loud shouts. **"Here I am, you horrible, awful person!"** It doesn't come bellowing in a parade down the Main Street of our lives, trumpets blaring, bright lights flashing, and a banner saying, **'Guilty. Guilty! GUILTY!!!'**

It whispers.

It slips in like a draft under your door in winter. It's subtle, sneaky, and deceptive. It's steals your peace and serenity.

> Mary would think, *'I should have handled this better.'*
>
> Or, *'I can't believe I'm still dealing with this.'*
>
> Or, *'I don't want to look at that bill yet.'*

Can you relate?

I know I can. When I would say or think something like this, I didn't connect it with a sense of guilt. It was what it was.

Yet, it's a close cousin, if not a member of the same immediate family.

Tied up in those thoughts is self-criticism. Waves of it. *"I should have handled this better"* is just another way of saying you didn't handle it properly to begin with.

Self-criticism.

"I don't want to look at that bill yet" is just another way of saying you can't deal with it yet.

Self-criticism.

When we think or say things like these, it's usually connected to delaying dealing with something (or dealing with it the *wrong way*), all to get some **short-term** relief from the discomfort it causes us.

While the financial situation may or may not get worse, the overall problem deepens because our self-doubt grows.

The loop begins again, getting deeper and deeper.

The excuses, the thoughts, the statements, the delaying, the ignoring… these are *all* about **self-protection**.

When you're critical of yourself or feel guilty about the situation you're in or the decisions you've made, your brain is dealing with the resultant **stress** of it all.

Stress piling upon stress.

As such, your brain shifts from problem-solving strategies to threat-avoidance. The goal -for your brain- is doing what feels better *now* (what offers immediate protection) rather than doing what's best long-term.

Avoidance or excuse-making provides an **illusion** of temporary relief, and that teaches the brain that avoidance "works," even though it's building the mountain of stress even higher.

The interesting thing about guilt someone feels is that it's meant to motivate them to do better next time, but it's actually perpetuating the vicious cycle that prevents them from moving forward.

Wouldn't it be great to have a friend, a companion who can remind you that you're doing okay? That there's nothing to feel guilty about now? That's Aarav The Serenity Genie™. And it's waiting to be that gentle support in Serenity Aligned™ (see back of book).

WHY GUILT FEELS LIKE DISCIPLINE

Is there any benefit to guilt? Many people are told that it can be useful.

The underlying concept is that discomfort pushes us to make changes or improve.

Yes, to some extent, I'll concede that guilt can make us desire to make a change in our life. Guilt *can* sometimes bring about necessary changes so we can be less stressed, less 'under the gun,' so to speak.

Guilt *can* be an effective way to help us realize there's misalignment in our life.

You may be asking, "Misaligned… *how?*"

Well, in any area of your life that isn't going in the direction you believe it should. This can be at a conscious or subconscious level.

- Some aspect of your moral fabric (ie. knowing right and wrong) could be out of alignment.
- Some part of your closest relationship (like a marriage, friendship, or among parents or a child) could be out of alignment.
- Some piece of your work ethic or output might be missing the mark.

So, yes, guilt *can* sometimes be a good thing… ***if*** it shows us *where* we are falling short *based on our own previously established expectations for ourselves*, ***and*** if we take that guilt and do something positive as a result.

When guilt is bad is when it becomes married to your psyche. That's when you're always feeling this way.

Constant guilt isn't about one aspect of life. Constant guilt mutates into the idea that something about *you* is wrong.

Do you see the difference? Does that make sense? Let's see if we can dig a little deeper and clarify this incredibly important point more.

Mary's ex-husband, John, had been paying the bills for years. He worked hard at a mid-level white collar job and Mary had returned to her career once the kids were old enough.

They had been doing okay, but with each small wage increase, they ended up spending more. On little things. Upgrading their phones, adding convenience or luxury to their lives, or buying a thoughtful gift that said, 'I was thinking about you today.'

Then John lost his job. He couldn't cover the bills and all the weight fell on Mary. At first, he didn't even tell her the truth. He kept getting up in the morning and left the house, pretending to work. Mary had no idea he was draining their savings and running up credit card debt just to survive each month.

John could have made a better decision. But he didn't and that led to more stress, a shorter temper, and eventually doubt that he'd ever get a new job. Mary then discovered what had been happening and it resulted in their divorce.

Feeling guilt wasn't solving anything for John or Mary. It was only keeping him from admitting to his wife what was happening. Just because he couldn't pay the bills anymore didn't mean he couldn't inform Mary of the truth.

It didn't help anyone. Guilt isn't going to help you, either. It only keeps us stuck in the self-deprecating loop that leads to bad decisions.

When money decisions are framed as **moral** failures, then every number you look at becomes a verdict. "Guilty!" it says.

Every mistake feels permanent.

Every setback feels *personal.*

That's not a recipe for hope. It's a recipe for fear.

And fear is the worst financial advisor you could have.

HOW GUILT ALTERS BEHAVIOR

Guilt. We all know the word. Many of us (or possibly *most of us*) have experienced it in some form or another at some point in our life.

Guilt for stealing something when we were kids. Guilt about cheating on a test or homework assignment. Guilt for breaking someone's heart. Guilt for taking advantage of another person's kindness or naivety or stupidity. Guilt for treating people different than us badly.

Guilt for not paying our bills on time, hiding truth from a loved one, or even ignoring a financial obligation, even to the point it goes to collections.

But constant feelings of guilt don't make people bad. No, it changes how they ***behave***.

It will make you:

- Delay a decision until you have no other option;
- Hide problems -even from the people closest to you- instead of addressing them early and getting ahead of the situation;
- Sway back and forth between over-control and avoidance;
- Abandon a 'good' system the moment it 'fails' you.

Most importantly, constant guilt is going to erode any trust or faith you have… in *you*.

If you constantly tell yourself you're bad with money, you will come to believe all your future decisions will be wrong, too. Why bother even trying then?

Why make a plan if you 'know' you're only going to fail? Why try to build a better management tool if you 'know' it won't stick because it didn't in the past? Why bother trying to pay your bills on time and pay down your debt if you haven't done it before.

Worse still, why would you want to look more closely at things if it's just going to confirm your worst fears?

Whatever happened in the past, whatever mistakes you made or things you avoided… it's done. It's over. And you need to let go of any guilt you feel. This is a core foundational principle of Serenity Aligned™ (see back of book): letting go of the past.

Yes, I know, it's easier said than done. But you're going to try. And Aarav The Serenity Genie™ is ready to help you each day, if you let it.

A BETTER WAY TO READ THE PAST

Millions of people around the world turn to 'mediums,' or people who claim to be able to read or predict the future to know what life has in store for them.

For us who are in some level of financial pain, knowing the future would be great, but our financial future isn't going to change *until* we deal with the present. And that means having to read the past. Not what lies ahead.

You need to not only change the way you think about yourself (as you relate to money) now, but also how you see the past. So, what I want you to do is begin reshaping your past. We're going to do that by **reshaping** your language, your word choices describing you and your past decisions.

Instead of asking: *"What's wrong with me?"*

Ask: *"What problem was I trying to solve?"*

For example, maybe you were trying to:

- Reduce stress
- Feel normal for a moment
- Buy time
- Protect someone
- Get relief from the strain
- Avoid conflict
- Survive a difficult season

When you make this soft, subtle change and see your past differently, those financial mistakes and decisions you keep beating yourself up over stop looking like recklessness. They start looking like what they were: ***coping***. Serenity Aligned™ (see back of book) is optimally suited to guide you in this subtle shift, to help you recalibrate *how* you think of the past and your current financial circumstance.

Humans change behavior more effectively when they feel understood than when they feel condemned[11].

That's the best way to reach serenity, and that's how we've decoded it. That's why we've developed Serenity Aligned™ (see back of book) to make opening it feel safe, not threatening.

RESPONSIBILITY WITHOUT CRUELTY

You have to take responsibility. You do.

But taking responsibility doesn't require punishment.

You can take ownership for your finances and your past mistakes and shortcomings without tearing yourself down.

You can acknowledge missteps without them becoming character judgments.

You can change patterns without hating yourself or even the version of you that created them in the first place.

Change has a way of sticking better when it's built on understanding rather than fear.

That's the difference with this book compared to most others on the market: responsibility with compassion.

11 Beyond punishment: The case for compassionate approaches in motivating behavioral change (Health Info Source). Nov. 5, 2024. https://healthinfosource.com/blog/beyond-punishment-case-compassionate-approaches-motivating-behavioral-change#:~:text=Accountability%20and%20punishment%20are%20intended,inspiring%20growth%20or%20positive%20change.

PERSONAL ACTION STEP 3: A PEEK INTO THE PAST

Take a moment to think about a past financial decision (just one) that you *still* feel bad about.

Open Serenity Aligned™ (see back of book) and write down that memory.

Now, complete this sentence (don't overthink it. Just be honest):

At the time, I was trying to solve: ________________________________
____
____.

Then complete this sentence:

What this tells me is not that I'm irresponsible, but that I was (i.e. maybe overwhelmed, maybe under-informed, maybe stretched too thin, maybe scared, etc.) ____
____
____.

Keep in mind that this isn't about rewriting history. It's about understanding and interpreting it accurately (perhaps for the first time in your life).

Aarav The Serenity Genie™, your personal companion on this journey (if you allow it), will use this to help you as it listens and learns and responds with gentle kindness.

WHY THIS MATTERS GOING FORWARD

What we're working on right now in these first chapters is removing

guilt from the equation. Because if guilt is driving your current decisions (even to pick up this book and start reading), then every plan you make, every step you take, every effort you put into change will feel heavier than it needs to.

Plus, every setback will feel much bigger than it is (and there *will* be setbacks… that needs to be understood).

However, when you push guilt out of the way, when you shove it down a cliff, send it toppling over a ravine into the rocks below where it belongs, you give room for understanding to come in. When that happens, a soft, subtle change happens, like the thin veil of light that breaks through thick, black clouds of an intense and long enduring storm… you feel relief.

You'll be more willing to look at everything.

You'll be more willing to adjust.

You'll be more willing to stay engaged, even when things don't go perfectly -or as planned.

This is where *real* progress begins.

Not with harsher verdicts or tougher rules.

Not with louder motivation.

With a calmer, clearer relationship with your own behavior.

Serenity. The Serenity Aligned™ (see back of book) way.

You don't need to punish yourself into a better financial life. You only need tools that work with how human beings actually respond to stress.

That's where we're going next.

CHAPTER 3

You Didn't Fail the System - the System Changed

You're not inconsistent; your environment is.

— — —

WHILE BASIC ECONOMIC PRINCIPLES HAVE REMAINED CONSISTENT throughout the ages, many facets of it constantly seem to change. We could liken that to changing clothing styles. As one generation ages, they connect less and less with those that come afterward, whether the differences are in musical preferences or dress or language.

A person in their eighties today might not be able to understand or relate to the financial challenges a person in their early twenties talks about.

Times change, my friend. So do strategies and tools that once worked.

For many people, one of the most confusing aspects of financial stress and strain isn't the stress.

It's the notion that something you *thought* would work -or that *should* be working- isn't. It's as though somewhere along the way, a change happened and you feel as though you're the only one who didn't get the memo.

I mean, you got *some* financial advice, right? It could have come from a parent or two, school, friends, a mentor, uncle, boss, or even something you read.

Yet even though you followed the advice and worked hard, dedicated yourself to 'moving up' in whatever profession you entered, and you tried to be responsible (the best you could), you still don't have stability.

You're still stressed.

Why?

You can't figure it out and the disconnect isn't just unsettling… it's nerve-racking. When the effort you put in doesn't produce the desired or expected results, the first place you'll tend to look is inward. You'll be confused. And you'll likely try to justify your failure, and when you can't find the reason externally, you'll probably blame yourself[12].

"I must be doing something wrong."

"I must have missed a step."

"I must not be consistent enough."

However, I want you to realize there's another possible explanation that doesn't get named often enough.

It could just be that the "rules" changed.

12 Andrew Quagliata. The Hard Work Fallacy: When Effort Doesn't Produce Desired Results (Andrew Quagliata). Aug. 11, 2023. https://www.andrewquagliata.com/post/the-hard-work-fallacy-when-effort-doesn-t-produce-desired-results

ADVICE THAT USED TO WORK

Too often, people get financial advice that doesn't actually apply to their circumstances. Sure, we can talk about managing your cashflow, and that's great, and keeping within your actual earnings, but so much of what we're taught was based on specific, consistent, measurable, and expected conditions.

- Steady income.
- Predictable costs.
- Clear career ladders.
- A more consistent relationship between effort and outcome.

Yes, there are plenty of people who have a steady and solid income. Yet, they've also experienced exploding costs, housing that far outpaced inflation and wage increases, food, entertainment, travel, and even the shift in technology and entertainment expenses. Today, streaming or satellite services are replacing the traditional cable television services, and each of those come with costs many of us simply don't pay close enough attention to[13].

In an ideal environment, specific strategies make sense. Being able to save and enjoy the fruits of your labors seemed attainable. Planning felt reliable, like a nice, warm pair of thick winter boots you could slip on when the snows fell and get out there and take care of the shoveling and clear your driveway.

What you may not have counted on were the mice that chewed the insides of those boots to pieces. Suddenly, your feet are sopping wet, freezing cold, and there's no way you can get the job done before you have to retreat inside.

13 Nu Yang. Global Healthcare Costs Projected to Rise More Than 10% in 2026 (World at Work). Nov. 13, 2025. https://worldatwork.org/publications/workspan-daily/global-healthcare-costs-projected-to-rise-more-than-10-in-2026

Today, there are 'mice' tearing apart the reliable financial advice and strategies. The assumptions we had about finances ten years ago are gone.

- Income is volatile.
- Costs rise unevenly and spike unexpectedly.
- Work is less linear.
- Financial security feels like it's connected to conditions we often can't meet.

When we take advice (it might even be great advice) that is meant for one set of conditions and try to apply it to another, then failure isn't personal. It's not your fault. Not completely.

It's contextual. Failure is based on the change of circumstances, conditions, and even unexpected realities.

WHY IT FEELS PERSONAL

When Jane's son Mark was young, he absolutely *loved* soccer (known as 'football' across most of the rest of the world). She bought him a ball to play with and a small goal with a net. He'd be outside for hours, learning to dribble, juggle, shoot, and run around. Jane enjoyed watching him practice.

Mark dreamed of one day playing professionally. The only problem was that he didn't know the proper way to shoot the ball, to dribble, and to move while approaching the goal. He also never played with other kids.

When he reached high school, it was natural for him to try out for the team. He had a growth spurt a year earlier and his solid four-foot-eight-inch frame suddenly shot up to 5-feet 5-inches. And he wasn't done growing. What this meant, though, was he struggled even more with basic soccer skills.

He never played on a team before because there just wasn't that option where he lived and he was shy, without many good friends. And he had been intimidated by the local teens and young adults who got together at local fields or even in the streets.

He didn't make the team his first year. He didn't even make it during the second year. He was devastated, but kept working at it. He tried different things. His basic skills improved a lot, but that was always at home, with no defense trying to stop him, no teammates to pass to.

The following year was met with the same results, the same disappointment. By the time he didn't make it onto either team his last year, Mark gave up.

He assumed he could never be good enough. And he carried that concept with him to other aspects of life beyond the soccer field.

Mark didn't even *think* about the impact just playing around by himself could have. At his house, conditions were optimal for making goals. No one watching him, no one trying to stop him, no one defending him…

In the world of competitive sports, that's not reality. And when it comes to our financial lives, that's the same concept: what we learn based on optimal 'safe' conditions is not reality.

In the real world, changes tend to happen gradually. It happens at such a snail's pace that you don't even realize things are shifting.

Then, many years later, you begin internalizing the conflict, determining that it **must** be because of something *you* did.

Hopefully you're the type of person who doesn't simply give up the first time you try something. Some people do; they quit after one try.

Most of us, though, tend to keep trying (to varying degrees). Basically, when you don't get something to work the way you thought it should the first time, you stop trying.

But what if you try repeatedly, only to end up missing the mark, to not get anything to go the way you *thought* they should go? We tend to then internalize.

Our response might be:

- *I'm not trying hard enough.*
- *I'm not disciplined enough.*
- *I'm falling behind because I did something wrong.*

Stop. S.T.O.P.

Stop Spinning Tires On Pavement (S.T.O.P.)

You don't go anywhere when your tires are just spinning around and around on the ground, when they never gain traction.

That's what all these responses equate to: going nowhere.

The **original** strategy/plan/mode of thinking isn't working with the current conditions.

Like Mark being thrust onto a field with other players, all trying to stop him from moving the ball or scoring, those conditions were not what he expected, not from his experiences while playing by himself.

None of this means that our efforts don't matter. Yes, they do. Your efforts are vital to success. However, you need to recognize that the playing conditions are different than what you expected or even different than they were in the past.

The rules change in the financial world. In the real world. In life. Let Serenity Aligned™ (see back of book) help you gain traction and calmness with encouragement and gentle support.

CONTEXT IS NOT AN EXCUSE

It's time to pause for a moment. Something needs to be made crystal clear here:

You are still responsible, no matter how much things change.

When we recognize that the financial system, or expectations, changed doesn't mean we can simply blame that and be done with it.

All this (about the changing system) explains some of the challenges and struggles many of us face, but it doesn't erase agency. What I mean by that is it doesn't remove our responsibility to navigate through these changing times.

If you're on a sailboat leaving Los Angeles and you're bound for Tokyo, that's a couple thousand miles across the open ocean. Going in a straight line makes the most sense, right?

But what if a storm blows up ahead of you? You need to adjust your heading (the direction you're going) to avoid it.

If you don't correct properly after the storm passes, you might end up hundreds or even thousands of miles away from your destination.

You still need to take ownership.

If you find yourself way off course (and you wouldn't be the only who has) you still need to take steps to get yourself back on track.

The tough reality, though, is that once you've made adjustments to your course, you can no longer use the same track you started out with. Aarav The Serenity Genie™ (see back of book) offers gentle, daily reminders, tips, and strategies that can get you back on course, no matter how far you drift.

With modern finances, you can't expect outdated assumptions or generic tools to work for your new course in life.

Fixed numbers are great, but what if your income isn't stable? What if it changes from month to month? Many small businesses face that conundrum regularly.

When you try to fit the outdated tool or system into your current reality, it's going to be tough, and it's going to lead to frustration. That only leads to unnecessary guilt, which compounds an already difficult situation.

When you understand ***your*** situation, that allows you to make better decisions about what tools and strategies are going to be most effective for you.

THE COST OF PRETENDING THAT NOTHING CHANGED

It's not too hard to imagine what happens when people are told that their struggles are all their fault. Most people respond to this by adding more effort–but that's rarely where the problem is. Then they completely disengage.

They give up.

Sometimes people will shift between one response and the other, trying harder for a period of time, then giving up, only to repeat the process for a while before finally letting 'give up' take hold.

You'll never find stability when you're operating in your life as though you're a ship being tossed around on rough seas.

All that's going to happen is the stress will run high, the pressure will mount, and your brain will seek out ways to find relief -even if only temporary.

Pretending that the environment around you (the financial situation, the economy, your family life, health, etc.) hasn't changed or couldn't possibly be the reason you're struggling isn't going to bring about something that holds under pressure in your life; it's only going to discourage you.

Discouraged people don't plan well. They react. And as we've kind of seen already, that reactionary state often feels like irresponsibility, but it's usually exhaustion taking hold.

WHAT ACTUALLY CHANGED (WITHOUT GETTING TECHNICAL)?

You don't need a technical degree to recognize that things are different in the financial world today. The global economy has grown. What happens in one country may have a direct impact on another.

The Internet, and social media in particular, has completely upended the way we receive information. That includes news.

People live-stream protests. Tragedies that strike are front-and-center news stories within minutes. Politics is a constant drumbeat in our ears. So is war, even if it's going on thousands of miles away and has no (direct) impact on our lives.

You don't think that can affect your finances? Or economics in your part of the world? It can, and it often does.

There's an old proverb that states if a butterfly flaps its wings in China, the weather in New York changes.

This means crises in some regions can affect other regions. The domino or ripple effect of conditions in one area can affect many others, and then those reactions can affect others down the line, and so on.

Like a tsunami, the wave can hit you directly. It can plow you right over, wash you underneath its power. Or its impact can be felt indirectly in almost innumerable ways.

Twenty years ago, Facebook was an infant and freelance (gig) work online was just finding its legs. Today, more than a billion people around the world work remotely as some form of 'gig' or 'freelance' worker. That type of work is definitely not going to offer a stable or steady income.

While inflation is generally an ever-present antagonist, recessions, depressions, and other factors can ramp up its rate of increase. Sometimes this can catch most people off guard.

Investing can feel risky, even though you watch various stock markets rise and rise and rise. Past crashes and crumbles and drops create a paralyzing fear; you don't want to trust what you see when it's growing because it just feels like it has to go back down.

Getting sick and suddenly realizing that your government or health insurance carrier or whatever doesn't cover the expenses can be frightening, especially when the cost is high.

These are all considered environmental stressors. They're not moral failures. And not having recognized this on the surface yet isn't about weakness.

It's just that you were trying to fit a square peg into a round hole. (You were trying to solve modern challenges with outdated solutions and strategies).

RECLAIMING SOME SENSE OF CONTROL

One of the most dangerous side effects of believing you "failed" is learned helplessnes14. This involves the quiet sense that no matter what you do, nothing's going to change.

That's a horrible feeling when you're in the midst of some tough financial times.

You reach a point where you don't even feel like getting up and going to work because, honestly, "What difference will it make?"

When a nation goes to war, it has choices. Whether it declares war on another nation or is defending itself, there are plenty of choices to be made.

One of the most critical -not just in the beginning, but throughout the campaign- will be deciding which battles are worth fighting and which ones should be left alone.

Most armies throughout history had to accept that some battles won't be won[14], so they focus on the ones they can win so that they have a chance to win the war.

You don't have to pretend that the situations you face or ideal, or that they are optimal. Just like a small nation that's been invaded by a much larger, more powerful one, you can gain some level of control by operating honestly within the conditions.

In order to do this, you must:

- Determine what you can control.
- Understand what's outside of your control.
- Where your energy will actually pay off best.

Aarav The Serenity Genie™ can help you determine these things daily, weekly, or whenever you need that assistance and calm, reassuring voice of reason.

14 Sun Tzu. The Art of War. https://classics.mit.edu/Tzu/artwar.html

PERSONAL ACTION STEP 4: CONTROL

In Serenity Aligned™ (see back of book) you will find there are two columns set up for this Personal Action Step.

The left column is labeled: **Things I Can Control.**
The right column is labeled: **Things I Can't Control.**

Then fill in those list. Remember, this is about your financial life, so let's try to focus and keep on task.

Some things you might list for being under your control might be:

- How well you track your money (in and out),
- What expenses you can prioritize,
- The pace you want to go at,
- Etc.

Some things you may list for being out of your control might be:

- The job market,
- Inflation,
- Housing or energy costs,
- Etc.

Spend a fair amount of time reflecting on **both** of these columns. When you're done, I want you to look at the second column and determine if you've been actively fighting any of those things.

Most of us do, and the more we do, the more energy we throw away on things we can't control.

The Serenity Prayer originally attributed to theologian Reinhold Niebuhr goes like this:

"God, grant me the serenity to accept the things I cannot change, courage to change the things I can, and the wisdom to know the difference[15]."

15 The original Serenity Prayer by Reinhold Niebuhr. https://proactive12steps.com/serenity-prayer/

Many programs designed to help people overcome challenges in life, including addictions and loss, use this prayer. They may use it as a prayer or simply a reminder that no, we are not in control *all the time*, and that's okay.

What's important is recognizing what we don't have control over and finding ways to still deal with them. Aarav The Serenity Genie™ is powerful at reminding us of those things.

MOVING FORWARD WITH CLEAR EYES

As we close out the first part of this book, it's important to be ready to move ahead with clear eyes, a clear focus.

I know it takes time (and effort) to change, even if it's just your thoughts and thought patterns, but beginning the process is vital.

And you've already done that. You've started.

Every journey, no matter how long, begins with one simple step: the first one.

You've already taken many steps, so let's keep moving forward.

In the next section, we're going to shift from context to comprehension. We're going to look at how stress, scarcity (even perceived scarcity), and human psychology interact with money in ways most people tend to ignore.

For now, it's enough to know that:

- You haven't imagined the strain.
- You're not weak because you feel it.
- And you're not stuck using strategies that no longer fit.

You're allowed to adapt. In fact, you *need* to.

Part Two

Money and Your Brain

CHAPTER 4

Your "Two Brains"

> *The moments you "can't explain" actually follow patterns.*

— — —

DID YOU EVER MAKE A DECISION AND THEN WONDER AFTERWARD, *'Why in the world did I do that?'*

You head to a local store to buy something simple. It might have been an 'everyday item,' something you needed, but a different item really caught your attention. You had the money but recognized that this wasn't the time to make such a purchase, and yet you did it, anyway.

Or you received a bill and though it was due in a few weeks, you had the money and could have paid it right then and there. You didn't. You wanted to wait. Then, when the due date arrived, you no longer had enough funds to cover it (because *maybe* you bought something you didn't need with those extra funds a week earlier).

You found a good book or information resource online that outlined a solid money tracking program or sheet or booklet, and you understood that starting earlier was far better than waiting, but you waited anyway. Another month. Before you knew it, three months had gone by.

Or maybe you had a financial windfall of some kind. A small inheritance or you sold an item you didn't expect would sell for what it did or received a bonus at work. Instead of paying down debts, you spent it on fun and pleasure.

Afterward, you thought, *'Why did I do that?'*

It happens to a lot of us. But that question *(Why did I do that?)* assumes there's only one version of you making decisions.

'Now, hold on a minute… I don't hear voices in my head,' you may be thinking. *'I don't have multi-personality disorder.'*

No, that's not what I'm getting at.

The human brain isn't one dimensional[16]. While the *overall* configuration of the map is multi-dimensional, what we're talking about here is how the brain processes information and makes decisions.

For the purposes of this book, our financial decisions are made by one of two 'brains,' or two ways in which the brain processes input.

Those two brains don't always agree, which is why you've likely had a few moments (more than a few, I'm sure) when you look back and wonder *why* you did what you did.

---

16 Behrens, Muller, et al. What Is a Cognitive Map? Organizing Knowledge for Flexible Behavior (Science Direct). Oct. 24, 2018. https://www.sciencedirect.com/science/article/pii/S0896627318308560#:~:text=We%20will%20also%20argue%20that,of%20all%20two%2Ddimensional%20spaces.

THE FAST BRAIN AND THE PLANNING BRAIN

There's a part of your brain that is fast. It's emotional and protective. This is the part of the brain that is built for survival.

It's this part of the brain that seeks escape when facing a threat (real, physical, immediate) or perceived (i.e., Stress).

The job of this part of your brain is to keep you safe. Usually that means safe *in the moment*. This part of your brain reacts quickly and prioritizes information into immediate concerns and those that can wait.

It's this part of your brain that is intensely sensitive to stress. So, when you're under stress, many of your knee-jerk reactions are going to be rooted in this part of your brain. It's just trying to keep you safe, even if it doesn't understand the 'threat' is merely financial or relational or emotional.

Yet, there's another part of your brain that operates slower. It is more deliberate in its calculations and decisions, and is focused on long-term aspects of whatever stimuli (or information) it's receiving[17].

This is the part of your brain that plans, weighs the pros and cons, determines tradeoffs to see if it's worth it, and focuses on longer timelines.

This part of the brain is the one that's active while you're setting goals, building tools or systems, or deciding what's best to do (for you, for your family, for your future).

Wouldn't it be great if we could all use *only* that brain when it came to money?

---

17 The Fast Brain System: Neuropsychological Framework (Creator's Friends). https://www.creatorsfriend.com.au/blogs/news/the-fast-brain-system-neuropsychological-framework?srsltid=AfmBOopXhsn4GGrvu_d7WL4C2LmmTehpLKVhWgZ8t60Bw9Ppbgjj1YOY

Unfortunately, we don't have the luxury of separating out these two 'brains' from one another. They are both essential for our survival and daily functions.

Neither one is broken.

However, they don't function under the same conditions. In a perfect world, life would be (mostly) calm and manageable. In that case, your planning brain would have room to work. You'd process information better, be able to manage your income more smoothly and easily, and wouldn't have to deal with interference (in these aspects) from the short-term protective part of your brain.

Yet, when pressure mounts, the fast brain takes over. It doesn't do this because it's irresponsible, but because that's precisely how it was designed to.

As I mentioned previously, it's not about responsible or irresponsible… it's a survival feature.

WHY STRESS ALTERS THE RULES

When you are under stress, your body *and* brain prioritize **immediacy**. This narrows focus. This also reduces tolerance for uncertainty. When there is any perceived uncertainty (real or imagined) while you're stressed, the fast brain is shoving that aside.

The goal, in this case, is to come to quick decisions that offer the most immediate relief.

As we've been discussing so far, some of those decisions that added to your financial struggles and challenges -decisions you *know* were not the best (or right) ones- came as a result of your fast, survival-oriented brain seeking relief.

Didn't it bring short-term relief?

Some of you are probably saying to yourselves, "Yes. Yes, it did." While others are still shaking their heads. Why? Because even though you may have enjoyed *some* immediate relief, that slower brain was still working, still processing, and knows that decision was only going to compound problems down the road.

When you're in real danger, that fast brain is powerful. And you appreciate it. But it's not as helpful when the so-called threat is financial pressure, especially when the struggle never fully gets resolved.

Money stress rarely feels urgent in the moment you're experiencing it. There's rarely one single dramatic moment. Rather, it builds to the point when urgent feels *'all the time.'*

Bills, balances, deadlines, broken systems, and uncertainty all keep your nervous system constantly activated[18].

When that happens, long-term thinking and planning becomes much tougher to do. Your 'fast' brain takes over, shoving the 'slower', planning brain aside where it struggles to be heard.

That only exacerbates the problems and the difficulties in life.

It's not that you forget what you learned.

It's that what you know feels less **relevant** than what you ***feel***.

HOW THIS SHOWS UP WITH MONEY

As we've started the second part of this book, the pieces are slowly clicking into place. You might be starting to see how confusing behavior starts to make sense.

18 Chu, Marwaha, et al. Psychology, Stress Reaction (National Library of Medicine). May 7, 2024. https://www.ncbi.nlm.nih.gov/books/NBK541120/#:~:text=Organ%20Systems%20Involved,atherosclerosis%20and%20compromising%20vascular%20function.

When you've had a bad day, you might have certain 'relief' behaviors that make you feel better -even if only briefly. Maybe on your way home from work who buy something at the market or mall or store, something you wanted but don't certainly need. Maybe you stop by a local watering hole

for an alcoholic drink. It's not because you 'need' one, but because it offers temporary 'relief.'

You may sit down with a stack of bills and decide to put it away until 'tomorrow' or the weekend or some later time -not because you're being careless, but because trying to sift through them all triggers discomfort and your 'fast' brain is looking for relief.

You may suddenly 'freeze' when it comes time to decide about something important -not because you can't (or are incapable), but because every option feels like taking a risk (whether that's true or not).

In every situation like this, the 'fast' brain is trying to reduce strain. It is trying to protect you. The 'slower' brain, the **planning** brain doesn't disappear.

It gets pushed aside.

Think about it like this: you have two young children. Perhaps they're six or seven years old. One is calm and poised, respectful and patient, willing to wait until someone calls on her. The other is hyper, boisterous and rude, constantly speaking out of turn, running around, seeking attention.

Which one tends to get a parent's or teacher's attention? The fast-moving, hyper, attention-seeking one, right?

That's kind of like our two financial brains. The fast brain is bouncing around, rude, and stepping in front of the planning, slower brain all the time.

When you judge yourself for that dynamic, it's not going to restore balance. Like the teacher who *knows* she shouldn't give all her attention to the hyper kid, but unless she finds a way to be proactive and deliberate in that action, it won't happen.

When you can't restore balance, it reinforces the stress you feel and that ends up giving your 'fast' brain even more control.

Now, if you were a parent of those two children and understood that the respectful, patient child deserved a chance to be heard, you would find a way to make that happen. You'd give her time to speak.

That's where we need to focus: *how* can we give our slower, planning brain time to move and process and be heard?

THE MISTAKE MOST ADVICE MAKES

I think most financial books and self-help guides and plans and courses and so on make one critical mistake: they *assume* that the planning brain is always available.

That advice simplifies the complex problems and says things like:

- "Just be more disciplined."
- "Stick to the plan."
- "Why can't you get this?"
- "Do what makes the best sense for you long-term."

That's all well and good (and advice most of us already *know*), but it's not going to help because the advice is **incomplete**.

That advice ignores the conditions under which decisions are actually made.

When someone is worn down, tired, emotionally frayed, and stretched thin, consistency is easy to say but harder to access. This isn't because you don't care. Actually, you care **a lot!**

It becomes harder to access because your cognitive resources are all being spent just trying to get through the day. You've got nothing left.

Expecting perfect or ideal long-term behavior from a stressed system is not realistic. Yet, that's precisely what much of the financial advice out there does.

When people fail to meet those expectations, they blame themselves instead of the mismatch or dichotomy.

You may be asking, "So why do so many people seem to get this right when it comes to money when they follow that other advice?"

Each of us is different. We all have unique experiences and expectations. Just as I told you not to go comparing your situation to another person's regarding finances or perceived success, don't make that same mistake here.

You don't know what someone else is going through. And I won't venture to try and navigate those complexities any further than to say some people quit smoking the very first time they try while others struggle for years and never quite get there. It's the same with other addictions.

It doesn't mean they're stronger or you're weaker; it only means you are different. And I would say they are more likely to be the anomaly than the average.

REBUILDING SELF-TRUST

Whenever you make a financial decision you later regret, that doesn't mean you neglected your future. Your decision-making process (and even logic) was operating under constraints.

The future felt too abstract compared to the present moment. When you can understand **and** accept that distinction, it will shift the solution.

If the problem were ignorance, then education would fix it. But that's not the problem.

If the problem were a character issue, punishment might help, but it doesn't.

However, ***if*** the problem is **stress**, then the solution isn't more information or tougher rules or more browbeating; it's designing systems that work *even when* you're under pressure.

Constantly telling yourself you should 'know better' erodes trust in your own judgment. Over time, if you keep breaking down the trust you (should) have in yourself, you'll stop believing you could make any good decisions at all.

When you lose trust in yourself, that's going to have more harmful effects than any single financial mistake.

The moment you understand ***and*** accept that different conditions activate different decision systems, something shifts.

You stop seeing your behavior as evidence of incompetence and start seeing it as *information.*

And *that* is information you can work with. Serenity Aligned™ (see back of book) is optimally designed to help you see that kind of information in your everyday life.

PERSONAL ACTION STEP 5: DECISIONS

Think of two financial decisions you made in the past year. They don't have to be monumental, but try for something more than 'everyday' decisions.

One of these decisions should have felt calm and considered while the other felt rushed, emotional, or stressful.

Enter a few notes about each one into Serenity Aligned™ (see back of book):

1. What was happening in your life at the time?
2. How tired or pressured did you feel?
3. What did you want most in that moment (relief, certainty, progress)?

Serenity Aligned™ (see back of book) will continue to build your profile and allow Aarav The Serenity Genie™ to patiently partner with you as you grow and change.

Also, don't evaluate the decisions yet. Just notice the context.

You'll likely realize that the difference between the two wasn't intelligence or values; it was bandwidth.

DESIGNING FOR REALITY

As we move forward, we're not going to try to silence the fast brain or shut it down. We're also not trying to get the slower, planning brain to win out every time.

The goal is to reduce unnecessary stress and build structures that support **better** decisions when stress is present.

That means we're going to be focused on fewer decisions, not more. We're going to clear out the defaults instead of constantly making judgment calls. We'll also try to push away systems that tend to catch you when energy is low. There's no need to demand more from you when stress is high.

We'll turn to those systems later.

For now, it's enough to understand that you are not inconsistent because you're careless. You are inconsistent because you're human, because stress changes how decisions are made. Once you stop fighting that reality, you can start working with it. That's where **real** financial steadiness begins.

CHAPTER 5

Scarcity Changes the Way You Think

Awareness is the first step, not the finish line.

— — —

Have you ever heard of a Chinese finger trap? It's a basic parlor trick these days, but it's an apt metaphor for what we're going to talk about.

A Chinese finger trap is a small tube, usually made from bamboo, that slips around two fingers (one on each end, usually the index fingers of each hand). You'd slide your two index fingers into the trap, one on each end, and then when you try to pull them back out, the trap engages.

The harder you pull, the tighter the trap. The key to getting your fingers released, then, would be to **relax**. When you gently push inward, the bamboo tube relaxes, allowing your fingers to slide back out.

It's kind of the same thing when you make decisions based on **scarcity**. The moment you do that, your 'fast' brain is working to find an escape. Not a long-term solution, but immediate relief from whatever pain or stress you're feeling.

When you're stretched thin, when you're under intense or simply constant stress, your brain will put forth a particular kind of decision. Well, that's the fast brain putting out that decision.

Your slower brain, the planning part of your mind, will be seeking a better solution, something that will result in longer-term relief, but that first part of your mind's processes will be shouting over everything else.

When you're stretched thin, being pushed to your limits, then you will tend to make certain types of decisions. Now, when I say, 'Being pushed to your limits,' I'm not saying you are at the bitter end or that your life is in real danger or that your house is about to be foreclosed on, your car repossessed, or you're contemplating something drastic or wrong… I'm merely saying to your ***mind***, you are stretched thin.

That's what happens to many of us when we're under financial stress without serenity. We feel *stretched thin*. We feel as though we can't take much more. We feel as though we're going to crack or crumble under this pressure.

And for our brain, it's designed to interpret that input as a very real and very immediate life-threatening situation.

Making decisions when you're at your wits' end or when you're pushed to your limits, or when you don't think there's any way out of the current situation isn't reckless. It's not careless.

It's urgent.

It's about survival. Sure, we've gone over this plenty; your life isn't actually being threatened, but your central nervous system **does not**

understand that. It is only operating based on the information it receives, and when you're stressed, guess what?

Your heart rate increases. Airways get expanded to increase the flow of oxygen into your body to feed the increased blood flow. Blood pressure ramps up. An energy boost happens[19].

When your body is reacting to stress this way (because your brain thinks there's a real threat against you), then the feedback loop tells your brain the threat remains, continuing the process.

Eventually, though, your body cannot sustain that on guard mode and you end up exhausted, fatigued, rundown, and energy depleted. Yet, your nervous system is still responding to the stress, continuing that (seemingly) never-ending loop.

As a result, scarcity tends to take center stage. Finances are low. Energy levels are low. Stress is overwhelming your system. Scarcity is the rule of law now[20].

When that happens, you will tend to choose the option that makes things easier 'right now.'

You may be fully aware that this decision will only make things harder down the road, but that doesn't matter to your overwhelmed brain. You may even tell yourself you'll 'deal with it' later on, when you have more mental bandwidth, when money comes in, or once things calm down. Like, when you're caught up.

But being "caught up" never seems to arrive.

---

19 How Stress Affects Your Nervous System (Lone Star Neurology, reviewed by Ramin Ansari). June 25, 2024. https://lonestarneurology.net/others/how-stress-affects-your-nervous-system/

20 Brendan Harkness. How to Avoid Scarcity-Based Thinking (Herox). https://www.herox.com/blog/741-how-to-avoid-scarcity-based-thinking#:~:text=When%20you%20feel%20pressured%20by,get%20out%20of%20the%20trap?

From the outside, this can look like a person being short-sighted, irresponsible, or reckless.

From the inside, it feels like survival. That's the impact scarcity can have on the way you think.

WHAT SCARCITY REALLY MEANS

When you hear the word 'scarcity,' what do you envision? Most people tend to think of deprivation. They might see people starving in a foreign country, their emaciated bodies, their eyes pleading for mercy.

You may think of poverty. Homelessness. People scrambling each day just to scrape by and survive, even if only barely. Maybe scarcity to you refers to lacking basic needs.

However, scarcity is personal. It doesn't have to mean you're barely surviving. It doesn't need to be absolute to be powerful.

Scarcity simply means not having enough of something that matters (to you).

Maybe to you, scarcity is defined as:

- Not enough money (even the 'rich' can feel like they don't have enough).
- Not enough time each day to get everything done that you need (or want) to get done.
- Not enough energy (you always feel drained by evening).
- Not enough cushion with your finances (you always seem to be waiting desperately for the next payday).

Whenever one of those (or similar) situations arise in your life, your brain interprets that sense of scarcity as a **real** threat, not just a perceived or imagined or middle-class or upper-class problem.

That's the moment your brain narrows its focus and priorities to the immediate. Its focus will be on finding a way to get relief **now**, not down the road, not in the future.

Now.

And one of the big, ***big*** problems we face today is that modern financial scarcity (real or perceived, based on the individual) is not temporary.

It lingers. It hangs on… for a long, long time. In some cases, it *never* seems to go away. When scarcity become chronic, it reshapes decision-making processes in subtle and persistent ways.

You probably didn't even notice the subtle change in your decision-making process at first when scarcity truly entered your life.

Perhaps you didn't notice any of those small changes that built, one upon another, until it reached a point where you didn't recognize yourself (or, at least, your own thinking) anymore (where it pertained to money).

HOW SCARCITY NARROWS YOUR WORLD

Operating under scarcity makes your 'world' a lot smaller. Narrower. Tighter.

The future doesn't disappear; it simply holds less weight. Less immediate 'relevance,' at least in your thought processes.

Trying to make long-term plans may feel like a joke when you don't know how you'll get through *today*. The entire concept of long-term thinking becomes too abstract for you. If you start to try and 'plan' for the future, it feels risky.

You make plans, goals, and lay out steps to get there, then the moment something doesn't work out or you miss your first target or two, the 'plan' suddenly feels further out of reach and desperation creeps in.

Do this a few times and you'll discover your decisions begin to lean toward speed over efficiency, certainty or possibility, or relief over growth.

Scarcity-based thinking will tend to drive us toward focusing on what's in front of us. We'll begin looking for immediate relief, short-term solutions, and even temporary reprieves, even if it costs us more over time[21].

From the outside, this often appears like poor planning.

From the inside, it feels like triage. In other words, it feels like you're on a ship that's taking on water while you run around plugging holes as fast as you can.

WHY "JUST THINK LONG-TERM" DOESN'T WORK

Well, we can say it works for *some* people, right? Just like the person addicted to nicotine or alcohol or drugs who finally decides to quit and does so without a hiccup, without ever slipping up, there are always going to be people who can do that.

Most of the rest of us aren't super-human. We're human. And we're flawed.

Sure, I could tell you to just think differently, but that doesn't remove the scarcity or the sense of scarcity.

That's what so much of the advice in the financial sector focuses on, statements and concepts like:

- *Be patient.*
- *Work out a plan and stick to it.*

21 Brendan Harkness. How to Avoid Scarcity-Based Thinking (Herox). https://www.herox.com/blog/741-how-to-avoid-scarcity-based-thinking#:~:text=When%20you%20feel%20pressured%20by,get%20out%20of%20the%20trap?

- *Delay gratification.*
- *Think about the future.*
- *Stay focused.*
- *Budget better.*

Not *one* of those statements, concepts, or ideas work well for most of us ***because*** we're human and we've gotten so accustomed to decision-making based on scarcity.

The longer you are caught in the scarcity-based thinking trap, the harder it is to get out of it[22].

Like the Chinese finger trap, the more you struggle, the tighter the trap becomes.

When scarcity-based thinking rules your life for years, the decision-making processes that have brought short-term relief (and the resultant feel-good neurochemical components like dopamine) become rooted in your life.

Scarcity interferes with good advice and counsel. You'll simply fall back into the 'feel good now' patterns, whether you want to or not, whether you even realize you're defaulting to that method of thought.

When your mental bandwidth is consumed by just managing what's right in front of you, there's less mental room left for abstract thinking.

It doesn't matter how good your planning brain is at solving problems; if your fast, reactive brain rules the roost, none of that other beneficial insight will see the light of day.

There's only so much attention your conscious thoughts can give to your brain's *millions upon millions* of calculations and processes every day.

22 Brendan Harkness. How to Avoid Scarcity-Based Thinking (Herox). https://www.herox.com/blog/741-how-to-avoid-scarcity-based-thinking#:~:text=When%20you%20feel%20pressured%20by,get%20out%20of%20the%20trap?

When you're walking down an unknown, rugged path in the woods, where do you tend to look? Just in front of your feet, right? You have to stop to look ahead and stop longer to look much farther ahead.

It's the same concept for your financial life, but in this case, your fast brain isn't giving you a moment's rest. Serenity Aligned™ (see back of book) is there to help your planning brain have the space it needs to operate properly by guiding you, reminding you, and encouraging you with calm, peace, and support.

HOW SCARCITY SHOWS UP WITH MONEY

Once you're able to recognize scarcity thinking, you will be able to see it played out everywhere. You may:

- Put off saving because today, money feels too tight.
- Choose to 'deal with' a late fee because not paying the bill now buys some breathing room.
- Avoid planning because plans have proven fragile to you.
- Tell yourself you'll start "when things improve."

Again, if you see yourself in *any* of these, it is **not** a sign of you being irresponsible. It's a sign that your system (way of thinking, etc.) is operating **under strain**.

This doesn't mean you don't have to take responsibility moving forward. You **absolutely do**!

But the strain keeps building. That's because scarcity-driven decisions only add to more scarcity. When that happens, it reinforces the cycle.

It's exhausting.

That has an emotional cost, too. This is one of the most overlooked problems of the scarcity mindset.

When you are constantly focused on the immediate, when it feels as though there's no long-term relief (only small fragments of short-term relief), life grows smaller.

You stop imagining what 'could be,' what 'might be.' You stop pushing yourself forward. You end up being cautious with some things, but hope dwindles in the process.

The future no longer becomes about something you build toward, but something to manage. As enough time marches on and you continue to operate in the scarcity mindset, a quiet resignation will gradually slip over you.

"This is just how it is."

We start accepting that things are what they are and they're not going to get better, no matter what we do, no matter how hard we try.

That's a dangerous place to get to.

Your expectations have become diminished.

This is the result of someone who is continually operating without any margin.

This has *nothing* to do with your personality. It has *nothing* to do with your potential. Scarcity thinking doesn't define who you are.

It's all about the state (of mind) that you're (currently) in.

Think about a time when you felt some *relief* from the constant scarcity mindset –whether it was about money, time, relationships, etc. When the pressure eases, even if only a little bit, what happens?

Don't you tend to become a little more patient? Don't you grow slightly more generous? Don't you begin thinking about the future a little more?

This isn't some phenomenal thing you've done. In fact, you didn't do it; this is merely **capacity** returning to your mind and body.

It's your planning, slower brain having time to process, room to evaluate, and bandwidth in which to operate.

When you're able to recognize this, it's going to change everything.

You won't fix scarcity thinking by admonishing yourself or berating yourself into better decisions.

You fix it by reducing pressure where you can and focusing on decisions that won't demand constant awareness.

LEARNING TO RECOGNIZE SCARCITY SIGNALS

Here we are, *finally*, to the moment when we start to take responsibility for our thoughts and actions.

You **must** begin noticing when you're working within a scarcity mindset.

Here are a few common signals that could indicate this for you:

- You feel rushed, even if there's no hard-pressing deadline. This can have to do with just about *anything* in your life: work, a project at home, dealings with a spouse or partner, etc.
- Even small decisions cause mental fatigue. Simply deciding on what to have for a meal when resources are limited could be a challenge.
- You default to a mindset of, "I'll deal with this later." And while most of us have done this, for you it may have become habitual.
- You choose certainty over possibility. This covers a lot of potential ground, but have you recently decided to choose something that wasn't the best for you just because it was easier?
- Maybe you have a conversation with your family about long-term topics, like future plans, and they start to irritate you.

These are just a few examples of the scarcity mindset creeping in on you. It doesn't mean you're failing, as I've stated before.

But when you begin to recognize these limits, that's the time where we need to think about stabilizing things, and there are multiple ways that we can do that, so let's talk about one shift that will start us down that road…

PERSONAL ACTION STEP 6A: A SMALL SHIFT

Right now, your goal should be to protect your energy.

If you're in a season of scarcity (whether it's real or perceived), you don't need to be dealing with finding a perfect long-term solution to your problems.

That's what most financial advice tends to push you toward: getting your long-term moves made now.

Maybe you tried to follow that advice already and it didn't work. This is why.

You need to find ways to reduce volatility. How do you do that? Well, **you shift your cognitive framework.**

We do that through a series of practiced steps.

- First, focus on **gratitude**.
  - This *doesn't* mean to be grateful for things you have no desire to be thankful for, but rather focus on what you *do* have. If we're constantly thinking about the things we lack (the scarcity), that's only going to spiral out of control. Instead, create a list of things you are thankful for and every day, focus on those things.
- Reframe your limiting beliefs.
  - If you keep thinking you'll never have enough (whatever it is), you're limiting yourself. Instead, focus on the resources you *do* have right now.

- Use 'Thought Stopping'.
    - This is pretty straightforward. When (not if, but when) you feel your thoughts spiraling down and down again, say out loud, "Stop." Who cares if someone hears you and doesn't have a clue why you just said that. Saying it out loud can have a powerful impact on diverting your attention *away* from the spiral.
- Focus on progress, not perfection.
    - I mentioned this previously… we're not looking for perfection. Humans are not perfect and never will be perfect. Stop expecting yourself to meet an unrealistic expectation. Instead, celebrate the small, incremental steps of progress. One day, you'll look up and realize how far you've come instead of constantly seeing how far you fell short of the 'perfect' expectation[23].

When you begin taking these steps, you'll be shifting your cognitive framework, which will move you toward less scarcity-mindset decisions and more reasoned, long-term benefit decisions.

Serenity Aligned™ (see back of book) offers the guidance and support you deserve to navigate these frameworks.

PERSONAL ACTION STEP 6B: PAYING ATTENTION

Wow. Already another one? Absolutely! Great job working on these.

Over the next several days, I want you to notice the moments when you feel rushed, avoid certain decisions or actions, or feel mentally overloaded by money.

23 McGarvie, Ph.D. 8 Strategies to Transform a Scarcity Mindset (Positive Psychology). July 15, 2024. https://positivepsychology.com/scarcity-mindset/

Keep track of them. Aarav The Serenity Genie™, your companion on this journey (if you choose to use it) offers a simple and convenient resource to help you monitor these feelings.

When you experience this, ask yourself one question:

Is this a scarcity moment?

As you contemplate these times when you experience them, you'll begin to notice how often they are actually rooted in the scarcity mindset.

This will indicate that something is happening to you rather than those actions or thoughts or decisions defining *who you are.*

Also, continue to focus on the four steps to rebuilding your cognitive framework (gratitude, challenging limiting beliefs, thought stopping, and focusing on progress, not perfection) every day.

This is the beginning of the revolution in your financial life.

MOVING AHEAD WITH THE RIGHT GOAL

You're not going to eliminate scarcity overnight. You're also not going to change your cognitive framework or stop your brain from reacting to stress differently in just a few days.

This is a process that takes time.

The goal right now is to stop misreading scarcity as personal failure and stop demanding long-term perfection from short-term capacity.

The present has been demanding too much of your time and energy to even *think* about the future properly.

And that's what we're changing now.

CHAPTER 6

Your Financial Style

Your money habits aren't personality — they're patterns.

— — —

No, I'm not going to quiz you or send you to some online portal for a 'personality test.' While there are certainly aspects to personality tests that are genuine, rarely do they tell the ***whole*** story (of a person).

What good would that do for us? None.

However, it's important to understand your ***financial*** style before we move on.

If you're like the majority of people in the world (it doesn't matter where you live, what country you call home, the economy, the fiscal structure, whether you're rich or poor or somewhere caught in the middle), you will have a specific way to describe yourself when it comes to money.

I'm not talking about describing yourself as rich or poor or middle-class. What I'm talking about is how you would describe the kind of person you are with money. Such as:

- "I'm not a numbers person." (In other words: I don't like math, so I deal with that as little as possible, *even when* it's important for my finances.)
- "I'm terrible at working with my money." (Or: I get caught up spending more than I know I should and hate confining myself to a set limit every month.)
- "I'm too anxious about money." (In other words: I worry about the bills all the time and haven't yet figured out a way to make my money stretch further.)
- "I don't worry enough (about money) –but I should." (Or: I know I should have this together by now, and though things get tight at times, I continue to kick the can further down the road).

Now, if you notice in my secondary examples, I gave an alternative concept, but one related to the quote. Yet, not everyone who says, "I'm terrible at managing my money" is indifferent or actually hates confining themselves to limits. It's simply meant to **expand** your thinking about these statements.

Too often, these statements or stories feel like identities. As though they're fixed traits and there's absolutely *nothing* you can do about them (or to change them).

We tend to think of these things as something we *are* or some characteristic we possess and that's it; you're stuck with them.

Whatever 'money personality' you possess, it's not a **personality**… it's a **financial style**.

A style is a set of learned responses that show up most clearly when you're under stress.

While it's difficult, if not impossible, to change your *personality*, styles can and often do change!

WHY THIS ISN'T A PERSONALITY ISSUE

This is incredibly important for you to understand: *however you describe the way you are with money* ***is NOT*** *about personality.*

It's about a style. A style you've developed and adopted into your life over time.

A personality trait is a label, and labels do little other than box people in and excuse behavior rather than explain it.

If I were to tell you that your financial situation is due to your personality, then there's really nothing we can do to change that. You're not responsible for it. All we could hope to do would be to develop tools and strategies that *might* help you work *around* your personality trait.

Hogwash.

No, a financial style doesn't define you. It isn't who or what you are… it's how you respond when money pressure increases. When stress rises.

When you respond to money stress, keep in mind it didn't come out of thin air. Your response didn't just magically happen. It was shaped by experiences.

It was shaped by what worked in the past, or at least by what *reduced* stress in the past, by what helped you get *through* difficult circumstances or a season of life. Whatever brought you some sense of serenity.

What I'm saying is that your financial ***style*** developed for a reason.

What we need to dig down to is *why* and *how* we developed that particular style. And Aarav The Serenity Genie™ is designed to help you discover your style and develop the one *you* want and deserve. It is a quiet mentor along this road and truly offers life-transforming guidance if you rely on it.

WHAT FINANCIAL STYLES TRULY ARE

A financial style or habit or behavior often develops and continues without us even realizing or thinking about it.

They are default coping strategies, or default financial patterns[24].

When life is stable, when money isn't tight, when things are going relatively smoothly, most people tend to behave in similar ways to each other. They are predictable.

However, when uncertainty creeps in, when stress increases because income fluctuates (i.e. independent contracting, freelancing, owning a small business, etc.), expenses rise (i.e. inflation), or some other stressor builds, other patterns begin to emerge amidst the noise.

- Some people pull away.
- Some people clamp down.
- Some people hope things will work out.
- Some people rush in to put fires out.

Not a single one of these *responses* is **irrational.** They're not. They are merely attempts by the individual to regain some measure of control or gain some level of relief using whatever tools feel the most comfortable (or easiest to use).

24 Jessica Medina. Dealing with Default Patterns: How Automatic Habits Shape Your Financial Decisions (Jessica Medina, LLC). https://www.jessicamedinallc.com/blog/default-financial-patterns-money-habits#:~:text=What%20Are%20Default%20Financial%20Patterns,with%20your%20broader%20financial%20goals.

The trouble begins when we start to think that those responses are *permanent* truths about who we are. When that happens, it's going to be exceedingly difficult to change how we think or what we do.

FOUR COMMON FINANCIAL STYLES WHILE UNDER STRESS

When you look at four difficult financial styles, you may likely see yourself in more than one of them.

That's normal.

The four financial styles we'll talk about are:

- The Avoider
- The Controller
- The Hopeful
- The Firefighter

We're not here to decide which one or multiple financial styles we fit into. We're here right now to notice the tendencies we currently gravitate towards.

Now, let's look at four financial styles.

The Avoider

I know this one quite well. When money stress starts pressing in, The Avoider seeks distance from it. They will often:

- Delay opening bills or bill statements
- Postpone decisions
- Avoid conversations about finances
- Tell themselves, 'I'll deal with it later.'

But you know what? 'Later' only comes when the walls collapse around The Avoider.

What often occurs, though, is that avoidance is labeled as irresponsibility. What's actually happening is that The Avoider has tapped into a strategy for reducing emotional overload.

Avoiding the issue buys temporary relief, especially when looking at their checking account, the bills pile up, and the debt that's mounting becomes overwhelming.

Some Strengths of Avoiders

There are some key strengths that Avoiders possess, such as **tending to remain calm in crisis.** They can also be quite adept at **creative problem solving**. After all, they must get that way to avoid the strain in the first place.

Also, when not threatened, they are often **capable of handling complexity** well.

Costs of Avoiders

Of course, there are also big costs to this type of financial style, most notably that **problems grow quietly**. When they finally explode, those closest to them are likely very surprised there were even problems to begin with.

Stress definitely lingers longer than it needs to.

Avoidance doesn't mean you don't care, but that you don't feel safe engaging right now.

The Controller

When The Controller feels pressured, they tend to respond by tightening their grip on things.

They may:

- Track obsessively
- Restrict spending aggressively
- Over-plan
- Feel anxious when things aren't precise

When living alone with no other dependents, friends, or anyone relying on you, this may not seem like a major problem.

However, when you're part of a unit, The Controller seeks to control *every aspect* of the unit's financial life. That often leads to a whole host of stressors beyond financial. It can cause strain in marriages, resentment from children, and much more.

Control creates a sense of safety. Knowing exactly what's happening can feel like protection against uncertainty. That may very well *feel* comfortable when money stress builds, but it doesn't improve the overall situation much.

There are people in the financial sector who praise this style. They see it as strong discipline to 'right the ship' of one's financial life.

For the individual and his or her loved ones, it's exhausting. It's unsustainable. And it's unhealthy.

Some Strengths of the Controller

Controllers tend to be organized. That's often praised in our modern society. And yes, being organized is a powerful asset in almost every situation.

They may also be proactive, seeking out solutions before problems develop too deeply.

Controllers also tend to be capable of maintaining structure even while under intense pressure.

Costs of the Controller

I think one of the biggest costs that Controllers face is **burnout**.

When you burn out, when you run out of energy, what happens? You quit. Or you explode. Nothing good will ever happen in those situations.

They also tend to be exceedingly rigid. There's no wiggle room. No compromise. And while that's not a major issue when you're on your own, when you're part of a team, family, or unit, it's a major issue.

Controllers are not flexible, so when flexibility is required, they struggle, and with a constantly changing world and technology, flexibility is almost essential.

The Hopeful

Wouldn't it be great if being eternally 'hopeful' was a powerful financial style? There are certainly benefits to being hopeful, but there are also costs.

Hopefuls cope with stress by focusing on possibility. (Isn't that a great thing?)

When money stress builds, they:

- Believe things will improve soon
- Delay tough decisions
- Focus on future solutions
- Downplay present constraints

For these people, hope is a survival strategy. It's not naivete. People learn to develop this style from past struggles. They learned that optimism is what keeps them going, keeps them moving forward.

Now, I don't want you getting confused here; 'The Hopeful' financial style doesn't mean everything works out for them in the end. That's not what this means.

It means they live more in a future *possible* world rather than in the immediate reality. So, they often avoid dealing with the financial problems of the moment like the other styles do, too.

Some Strengths of the Hopeful

Hopeful people are future oriented. This can be a wonderful thing, especially if it helps to shift their decision-making processes from short-term to long-term.

They can often be resilient. No matter what gets thrown in their path, they continue to get back up, climb over the obstacles, and keep pressing onward.

These people constantly imagine better outcomes, and that can definitely be a positive thing.

Costs of the Hopeful

There are generally many missed opportunities that Hopefuls watch slip by that could have helped them stabilize their financial life.

They tend to hit the 'reset' button over and over, which doesn't move them forward. They are mostly focused on 'later' to solve 'now' issues.

Hope can work, but only if it's paired with structure.

The Firefighter

When most people are running away from fires, there's a type of person running *toward* them. We mostly call these men and women 'firefighters.'

They're often thought of as heroes, too, right?

Well, when money stress increases, there's a financial style we'll call The Firefighter. They:

- Tend to jump into action
- Make fast decisions
- Solve immediate problems
- Worry about consequences later

When you are constantly staring down the barrel of a loaded crisis, this style might emerge. That's because when you're constantly under financial strain, acting fast seems necessary.

While the Firefighter isn't protecting anything, but only putting out fires, it's going to be difficult to keep this pace up for too long. Something's bound to give out.

Some Strengths of the Firefighter

For the most part, in our discussion, 'Firefighters' tend to be decisive. They are faced with a critical situation and take charge.

They can be resourceful, but within the limits of the circumstance. In emergencies, this financial style will be fairly effective, at least where it pertains to alleviating financial strain.

Costs of Firefighters

Imagine a real firefighter *constantly* rushing into burning buildings, lugging massive hoses up many flights of stairs, and under threat of harm. Wouldn't that get exhausting?

Yes, and that's what happens as a result of this type of financial style.

Any short-term solutions this person would come up with will only create more long-term strain. This style also means people struggle to transition out of crisis mode (even when there is no crisis anymore).

When everything feels urgent, nothing gets to be strategic. Any long-term planning simply perishes in the wind.

You can reference these financial styles at any time for reminders and help navigating your own through Serenity Aligned™ (see back of book).

WHY YOUR STYLE MAKES SENSE

The financial style you fit into best didn't emerge by random chance. It didn't just 'appear' one day in your life.

It developed over time.

It was reinforced by even more time.

Somewhere along your journey in life, especially when you became at least partially responsible for your financial well-being, responding the way you did reduced stress.

It gave your brain that shot of dopamine, that 'Ahh' moment that helped you breathe a little easier for the time being. Maybe even those decisions helped you survive a difficult season in life.

Your brain noticed. Not that part of your brain associated with planning, organization, and long-term future details, but the quicker, survivalist part.

Believe it or not, this financial style may have fit your life at the time. Clearly, there was a need for it somewhere in your past.

The problem now is that it no longer fits your current circumstances. It doesn't meet your current reality anymore.

Whatever worked when things were not stable won't offer the same results when your financial situation improves or changes.

When you can recognize that reality, you can begin to climb out of the trap you've fallen into.

When you take that financial *style* and confuse it with your *identity*, you're going to have problems.

When this becomes your identity, you shut down other options, other possible ways to get out of the situation you're in.

When behavior becomes identity, change feels fraudulent. When you believe that this style is your identity, then any attempt to fix it from the outside will make it feel as though you're *pretending* to be someone else.

That rarely ever sticks for long.

I want you to step out of the concept that this is your *identity* and instead recognize it's only a **style**, one that you can change.

More importantly, strategies and tools can work with different styles. They might simply need tweaking.

You can't say the same for identities.

THE REAL GOAL: STRATEGY THAT FITS YOU

Now that we're really getting into the thick of things here, I hope you can start seeing and understanding why so much of the other financial advice you've heard or accepted or tried in the past didn't work.

They assume one ideal way of behaving. They assume styles are actually behaviors or, worse, that no matter what identity or what style you have, you can simply change it by *willing* it to be so.

That's not how the human psyche, brain, or behavior works. That concept goes against nearly every psychological framework and understanding to date.

For some people, those stock, standard strategies work. But not for all. Not even close.

In order to change our behavior in a way that lasts, in a way that sticks for the long haul, it must first align with how we *naturally* respond under stress.

- An Avoider doesn't need more spreadsheets… they need safer entry points.
- A Controller doesn't need tighter rules… they need flexibility without fear.
- A Hopeful doesn't need less optimism… they need grounding.
- A Firefighter doesn't need more urgency… they need recovery and structure.

Friction is typically what causes systems to fail. Think of a car's engine. When you have the proper oil in it, the cylinders don't overheat. The components run smoothly and you can get where you need to go.

However, without proper lubrication, friction increases, as does the heat, to the point when the entire engine can seize up and stop moving altogether.

Our goal is to reduce friction by finding a strategy that will *match* your financial style best.

PERSONAL ACTION STEP 7: FINANCIAL STYLE

Take some time to reflect on your **financial style**. Fill in the following thoughtfully in the Serenity Aligned™ (see back of book) app:

When money stress increases, I tend to ______________________________
____.

This helps me by ____
____.

This costs me by ____
____.

There's no need to pick just one answer. But what I want you to do is look for the patterns.

WHAT COMES NEXT?

We're not going to solve our money problems by just acknowledging we have a specific style when confronted with money stress. Hopefully, though, it'll change how you approach solutions.

When you start designing systems that support how you actually behave, then the changes become more natural. They *feel* better, not as forced.

When something doesn't feel forced, you end up holding on to your energy better.

I don't need you to *be* better. Your family doesn't need you to *be* better.

This is about **building** better around *who you are*.

Willpower can certainly carry you so far, but for most of us, that's not far enough to bring about lasting change and forward progress. Not in a constantly shifting landscape of financial circumstances.

Job insecurity, income fluctuations, inflation, etc. all conspire against stability, and we're focused on adapting to be prepared for whatever the future throws our way.

CHAPTER 7

Patterns, Not Willpower

Willpower fails — systems don't.

— — —

MICHAEL WAS A FORTY-SIX-YEAR-OLD MIDDLE MANAGER AT A RATHER large company. There was no risk of this business being mistaken for a Fortune 500 company, but it employed a few thousand people.

Being middle management, Michael had a decent salary. He was earning a lot better money (now) compared to when he first started straight out of college. He was married with two children, had a house in the suburbs, and seemed to be doing fine from the outside.

In reality, Michael and his wife Emily were stretched thin. The more he earned, the more raises he received through the years, the more they spent. Their small, one-bedroom apartment became a two-bedroom house, which eventually led to their current four-bedroom, three-car garage house in an upscale community.

It wasn't just the house, either, but the cars, the vacations, the clothing, and electronics, toys, video games, and more that they bought for themselves and their children.

They were considered "upper-middle-class," but they were still living paycheck to paycheck. They also took care of both sets of parents. For them, that was a responsibility and a privilege. And, at the time, their debts were manageable and things were going relatively smoothly.

Then something happened that shifted everything. Inflation skyrocketed in one year. The cost of groceries almost doubled. Electric rates soared faster than they imagined they could. Before he knew it, Michael was juggling bills, frantically striving to balance his flow of money at that time.

For the most part, Michael was working 10 hours a day, five days a week, and then spending his Saturdays doing work around the house, spending time with the kids, then Sunday, which used to be his day of rest, he found himself immersed in a wide range of projects for work, more obligations with his family (as the kids got involved in more activities), and feeling like there was always something to do.

It seemed as though he didn't have time to do *anything* anymore. So, when it came to his finances, he started saying to himself, *"Next month, I'll do better."*

For the next two years, *"Next Month"* never came.

At some point, most of us have made this type of promise to ourselves, a promise that we are going to ***do better***, not just now.

We may not have the bandwidth to deal with the problem(s) at hand. Perhaps we just couldn't handle the stress with everything else going on in our life.

It may have been a promise to:

- Track your expenses more closely.
- Have that conversation with your partner or spouse you knew you should've had months ago.
- Get more disciplined.

Maybe for a while you managed. You did **exactly** what you said you would do. Or maybe, if you're like me, a lot of those promises slipped by the wayside almost as quickly as you made them.

Life has a habit of 'getting in the way.' The things you assumed you would 'get to' have to take a backseat to 'survival.'

Maybe work gets busier than you expected it would. Perhaps an unexpected situation arose, like the death of a loved one, an illness, or financial crisis beyond your control. Everything you built, everything you carefully constructed based on your current earnings began to fall apart. Then, when you make that promise to yourself that you'll get on top of this *next week or next month* became tougher and tougher to do.

When you miss one opportunity, guilt seeps in. Then, when the second opportunity passes by, motivation fades.

Eventually, the whole thing quietly collapses.

When that happened for Michael, he didn't blame the system. He didn't blame the financial system that he and his wife had built and relied on for years; *he blamed himself.*

Most of us tend to do that. **We blame ourselves.** It's easy to do, isn't it?

We say things like:

- *I just don't have the discipline.*
- *I can't stick with anything.*
- *Other people must have stronger willpower than I do.*

Believe it or not, willpower has **never** been the real engine of progress. It's something a lot more perfunctory than that.

THE MYTH OF MOTIVATION

In our modern age, no matter where you live, 'motivation' is a topic of endless discussions, speeches, programs, coaching, and more.

'Motivation' is the core of almost every self-help book, guide, program, and conference you can possibly imagine. And it's what promises success or peace or even serenity.

Unfortunately, motivation is *unpredictable*. Sure, it sounds great in a speech, on a placard, or a poster, but motivation is fickle. It can come and go like dust in the wind.

When something feels new, motivation can be strong. Or when something is urgent, motivation might spike. When the novelty of this new plan or system wears off, when stress rises, it can fade just as quickly.

That is merely how human attention works. It's not a flaw. It's not some character flaw that you possess when you can't seem to hold onto motivation for longer than a commercial break of your favorite television program. It's just human nature.

Most of the financial advice you've likely heard before is built on the foundation of motivation. This assumes that motivation is stable, that your consistency can be infinite.

All this advice assumes you can:

- make good decisions all the time
- resist temptation indefinitely
- apply effort evenly across every session of life

When you're faced with real world conditions, real-world stress, that assumption is going to collapse quickly. This gets exacerbated when you're tired, worn out, and exhausted. As I've mentioned previously, you are only human. You can only do so much. Stop beating yourself up about it.

Willpower ***is*** going to fail under pressure. Sure, we can sit here and point to a list of examples of people who *seem* to have willpower that presses on, even if (or especially when) the "pressure is on" constantly. Athletes, political leaders, business executives, and more all ***seem*** to access some mystical ability to maintain strong willpower, perhaps especially under pressure.

But willpower is not a personality trait. **It's a limited resource**[25]. There's only so much mental energy you have each day. There's only so much you can accomplish, and that goes for not just your physical abilities, but your mental and emotional abilities, too.

Each decision you make every day — whether it's related to work, family needs, social interactions, what you need to buy or skip, etc. draws from the same pool of mental energy.

The moment that source of mental energy runs low, your brain begins looking for shortcuts. This is the moment when:

- impulse purchases feel justified
- avoidance feels safer than engagement
- long-term plans feel optional

None of this means you stopped caring. Your system has just depleted. All that wonderful, feel-good motivation that you started with **evaporates**. Then, you're not only left with the same problem to deal with, but you start looking *inwardly* for excuses and begin blaming yourself.

25 What you need to know about willpower: The psychological science of self-control (American Psychological Association). Jan. 26, 2012. https://www.apa.org/topics/personality/willpower

If you expect that you can override exhaustion with fortitude, that would be like expecting your cell phone to continue working even when the battery has been completely drained and you don't plug it in to recharge.

The problem you're dealing with isn't commitment. I know you're committed to making these changes. The problem is your capacity to handle all these different things at the same time is limited.

So, why does repeated failure feel personal?

Well, when systems begin to fail, people tend to internalize the breakdown.

Likely, you:

- assumed the rules were fine,
- assumed the plan was solid,
- assumed the only weak link was you.

When this goes on long enough, trust in yourself begins to erode. Like the constant pounding of the ocean surf on the shore, it is going to erode the sand dunes, the wooden piers, and everything else that gets in its way.

You can build a strong wall intending to hold back the tide, but eventually the ocean (*and* the storms) is going to win out, in time.

When our self-trust, when faith in what we can do erodes, we have a tendency to stop believing our future intentions even matter. Quietly, we stop starting things because we don't trust ourselves to finish them.

'What's the point in even trying,' you start thinking, 'since I'll never finish it, anyway?'

What happens next? It's actually an interesting thing… that belief becomes self-fulfilling. Because you never get going on making changes, you continue to point to yourself and think, *'See? I knew nothing was ever going to change.'*

But, by that time, you've given up trying, and yet still blame yourself for *not* trying.

This is how so many people get stuck in the cycle of starting and restarting and then giving up, only to sort of start or restart, instead of progressing.

PATTERNS WORK WHEN WILLPOWER CAN'T

We are now getting to the crux of this chapter, which is about to lead us into second half of this book where real change is going to take place.

Here is the key shift you'll need to make:

Stop thinking progress comes from wanting it more. If that were the case, you would already have made progress. But you haven't, have you?

Progress comes from needing less effort to sustain it.

What we are talking about here is a **habit**.

Habits reduce decision-making. When you have a bad habit, for example, what do you do? You begin doing that behavior — whatever it is — without even thinking about it.

Habits, or patterns, remove friction. They make the "right" choice the *default* voice, instead of a constant negotiation you're making with yourself every day, every hour, or every minute.

When something is habitual, it doesn't rely on your mood, your energy level, or any external factor that's going on in your life. It just happens. Naturally.

Of course, habits don't happen 'naturally.' They are the product of *small things done regularly.*

Patterns matter much more than motivation, especially when it comes to money. When decisions need to be made frequently and can often overload emotion, patterns keep us grounded in doing what is right.

ENVIRONMENT SHAPES BEHAVIOR MORE THAN INTENTION[26]

What I'm about to say is perhaps one of the more uncomfortable truths we have to confront if we are to create lasting change in our financial lives: *your environment influences your actions more than your values do.*

Let me repeat that:

Your environment influences your actions more than your values do.

Your values already dictate that saving is more important than spending, but if spending is easy and saving is hard, you'll spend more, *regardless* of your intention.

You know it's important to check your balance and make sure you have the money for whatever is coming up (bills, a vacation, something you want to buy, etc.) but if checking those balances creates anxiety, your brain will want to avoid it, regardless of your intent to be responsible.

Even though you understand doing the right thing can be hard, if each decision requires active effort, that's exhausting and your brain will desire for you to choose relief, even though you know the right thing to do.

Your environment is a greater factor on your actions than your values.

---

26 Duke Today Staff. Key to Changing Habits Is in Environment, Not Willpower, Duke Expert Says (Duke Today). Dec. 13, 2007. https://today.duke.edu/2007/12/habit.html#:~:text=According%20to%20a%20Duke%20University%20psychologist%2C%20almost,food%20*%20The%20location%20*%20Physical%20locations

You cannot will yourself to become a better person just because you want to be. You must rearrange the environment so that the desired behavior requires less effort.

This all comes down to reducing friction so that the biggest changes can take root.

It's easy to assume that change requires drastic action. That's where most financial approaches and systems fail. We focus on unique, drastic, dramatic changes to be made right out of the gate.

For some people, this can work. For most of the rest of us mere mortals, it usually doesn't help in the long run. It only sets us up for failure, leading to self-doubt, guilt, and a lack of self-trust as we've mentioned already.

Small adjustments — what behavioral scientists call ***friction*** — can have greater, outsized effects[27].

This means *adding* friction to unwanted behaviors. For example:

- Removing saved payment methods.
- Logging out of shopping apps.
- Delaying purchases for 24 hours.

When you *add friction* to these unwanted behaviors, you force your brain to have to deal with a very simple truth: to get the desired relief, it is going to require more effort, forcing your brain to question whether this is going to fulfill that role.

When you remove saved payment methods, that means any time you want to purchase something from your phone or laptop you have to dig out your credit card, enter the information in manually, and this creates *more friction.*

27 Friction Adjustment (Sustainability Directory). Nov. 10, 2025. https://lifestyle.sustainability-directory.com/term/friction-adjustment/#:~:text=It%20is%20the%20art%20of,default%20path%20of%20least%20effort.

When you delay purchases by just 24 hours, your brain is no longer getting that immediate dopamine hit by purchasing something you wanted in the moment. If you still want that item, even though it may hurt financially, then you must deal with that later, but you have added friction to the process, removing the immediate (perceived) reward.

Aarav The Serenity Genie™ is designed to help you create or reduce friction, when you need it.

What about removing friction from helpful behaviors? For example:

- Automate transfers from checking to savings every paycheck.
- Simplify your accounts.
- Set reminders that won't create guilt.

As you can (hopefully) see, none of these changes rely on willpower. They work whether you're tired or full of energy. **This is where real progress begins to gain traction**.

WHY "TRYING HARDER" OFTEN BACKFIRES

When you 'try harder,' it increases pressure. When Michael (our example at the beginning of this chapter) was trying harder, it only added pressure, which narrowed his thinking. This meant an increased chance of making mistakes. Then, when he made mistakes, it only increased the feelings of guilt he had been dealing with.

When you feel guilty, it makes everything harder.

When you care deeply about your finances, you ***will*** struggle the most. That's just the nature of this beast. People who don't care about their finances will **not** struggle. But *you care*. So, you'll struggle.

You put a tremendous amount of emotional weight on every single decision. This drains your energy faster and faster and increases the likelihood of burning out.

When you focus on a kinder, gentler system, like adding friction to unwanted behaviors and reducing friction from helpful behaviors, you are creating a more efficient system that is set up to help you... *based on you,* not someone else.

DESIGNING FOR LOW-ENERGY DAYS

There are days when you have a lot of energy. And there are plenty of days when your energy reserves are low.

You already know this. You understand how energy ebbs and flows, rises and drops. You can't control this very often; it's the result of emotion, circumstances, and environment.

When you want to build lasting financial patterns that help you, one of the most important questions you need to ask is: *"What will I do on my worst days — not my best ones?"*

Most financial advice you've heard to date assumes you will be doing this on your best days. That is *not* where most of our problems arise.

A system that is built for *only* when you're motivated is a fragile system. A system that will work, even when you're tired and drained is one that can be sustained.

This might mean creating smaller automatic transfers instead of big, ambitious ones. Maybe you have grown into the habit of making manual transfers from checking to savings or investment accounts, but now I'm telling you to automate those, but focus on smaller numbers to start.

Small successes can lead to big celebrations.

Maybe, when tracking your income or spending habits, focus on fewer categories instead of many hyper-detailed ones. This prevents mental overload.

Instead of daily scrutiny, focus on weekly check-ins.

By lowering the bar, this doesn't mean you are lowering your standards, it's simply starting the process of **building patterns** you can take with you even when (and especially if) energy levels are low and challenges high.

PERSONAL ACTION STEP 8: BEHAVIOR

Choose one financial behavior you want to make easier for yourself.

I'm not talking about doing something perfectly, just easier.

Ask yourself:

What makes this behavior hard for me right now?

What could remove one small obstacle?

Here are a couple simple examples to help you start thinking along these terms:

1. Maybe you can automate a bill you tend to forget.
2. Perhaps you can set a calendar reminder that feels neutral, not scolding.

Ultimately, the goal is to simplify where your money flows *when* it comes in.

Then, pick **one** change. *One change only*. And implement it. Stop there.

Momentum will come with accumulation, not the intensity with which you start. Aarav The Serenity Genie™ listens, too, which is what will help you focus on the right behaviors you want. Enter this information into Serenity Aligned™ (see back of book) and you can get gentle, daily reminders about this change. You can also ask questions in the app to get clarity.

If you slip, there will be no judgment, only a calm, supportive listening app that helps you get back up and take another step.

THE RELIEF OF LETTING SYSTEMS CARRY THE LOAD

When habits and systems are doing their job, something subtle but important happens. You stop negotiating with yourself all the time. You stop turning every decision into a referendum on your character. You conserve energy for things that actually matter.

Financial steadiness isn't about white-knuckling your way through every choice. It's about building structures that hold when you don't have much left to give.

As we move into the more practical chapters of this book, this principle will keep showing up:

- If a system requires constant perfection, it will eventually fail.
- If a system reduces friction, it has a chance to last.

You don't need more willpower. Whatever you thought about a lack of willpower or failure in this aspect in your life in the past, let it go. Let it stay in the past. You don't need to be tougher on yourself.

You need systems that respect the reality of fatigue, stress, and limited capacity. That's something we are designing… **a system for *real life*.**

In the next chapter, we're going to look at one of the most misunderstood behaviors of all: emotional spending. We will learn how awareness, not restriction, is what actually leads to lasting change over time.

For now, though, it's enough to remember that when you're tired, patterns matter more than intentions and building better habits starts with kindness towards your own limits.

CHAPTER 8

Emotional Spending isn't Stupidity

Emotional spending isn't foolishness. It's communication.

— — —

MARY WAS JUGGLING TOO MUCH JUST TRYING TO MAKE ENDS MEET AS a single mom. Every day was a struggle. Most evenings, after cleaning up dinner and having her kids finish their homework, take a shower, and get ready for bed, she would sit on the couch in the family room, her fingers gently cradling a glass of wine, slowly swirling it as she stared at the liquid rolling in a gentle pattern, wishing her life could feel as smooth as that drink.

Her thoughts would run in a million different directions at once, but it always seemed to come back to the same starting point; she would ask herself, "*Why did I do that?*"

On her way home from work, rushing to meet the kids as they got off the bus, or while out shopping for groceries, she would notice an item on an end cap, a special display case, or some 'Super Sale,' and just "had to purchase it."

It's not like she had extra money lying around because her ex, John, wasn't sending any.

It's not as though she was rich and could just buy whatever she wanted at any time.

It was because the purchase made her *feel good.*

Most of us know this feeling. We've done it. We have talked about this already.

Even though Mary might not have understood the neurochemical reaction that happened in her brain because of those purchases, it was something that made her feel good for a brief time. It alleviated stress, even if only temporary, and even if it added to her financial struggles later.

When we purchase something and feel good, the tension in our life eases. Maybe you don't even purchase something for yourself, but for your spouse or partner, best friend, or child. The goal is for them to love it. You want to bask in their reactions, as though it was your reaction.

Whoever the purchase is for, it brings a sense of satisfaction. *It eases tension.*

Suddenly, the day feels lighter. The constant noise of stress and anxiety quiets, if only temporary.

After some time passes, the feeling also passes. In the vacuum of that feeling evaporating comes not relief, but judgment. You start thinking, as Mary did:

- *Why did I do that?*

- *I didn't even need this.*
- *What is wrong with me?*

Emotional spending is commonly associated with either a lack of intelligence or a lack of consistency.

It's neither of those things.

If you listen to much of the financial advice on the market today, you will read or hear that emotional spending needs to be controlled and stamped out of your life completely. Why?

Because all of those other books and courses and advice and information label emotional spending as *stupidity*.

It's not.

Emotional spending is **communication**.

WHAT EMOTIONAL SPENDING ACTUALLY IS

When we use money to regulate feelings rather than to solve a problem, especially a financial problem, that is emotional spending.

Whether it's because we feel sad, are anxious, are lonely, bored, or

whatever, the spending is not about necessity. It's about finding temporary comfort[28].

It may seem harmless at the time we're doing it, but it often leads to regret and guilt.

28 Emotional Spending -Why We Shop When We're Stressed (Road to Therapy). June 17, 2025. https://roadtotherapy.com/2025/06/17/emotional-spending-and-mental-health/#:~:text=What%20Is%20Emotional%20Spending?,us%20with%20regret%20and%20guilt.

Have you ever experienced a time when you bought something you didn't need, couldn't really afford, or just did it on impulse when you were feeling:

- stressed
- fatigued
- lonely
- frustrated
- bored
- needed comfort
- or needed to feel "normal?"

During times like this, the purchase is hardly the point. It rarely is what matters under the surface. The purchase creates a neurochemical reaction in the brain that releases dopamine, endorphins, and other 'feel good' hormones and chemicals that help us alleviate the perceived threat that is found bound up with stress[29].

When something feels off, humans look for relief. Money is one of the most accessible tools we have at our disposal that can create quick relief, even if it's only temporary and even if it's going to confound problems later on.

WHY EMOTIONAL SPENDING FEELS SO CONVINCING

As we detailed quite clearly in the first part of this book, your brain is seeking relief from stress as quickly as possible.

29 Money Mindset: Understanding Emotional Spending & Ways to Overcome It (Mary Rigg Neighborhood Center). https://www.maryrigg.org/money-mindset-understanding-emotional-spending-ways-to-overcome-it/#:~:text=Emotions%20can%20influence%20our%20spending,well%20as%20happiness%20and%20celebration.

If you remember, there are two aspects of your brain at work when you're stressed or anxious: what we call the fast brain and the slow, planning brain.

Most of the time your primal, or fast, brain wins out because its desire is to gain relief from whatever perceived threat there is.

When you're stressed, your brain is seeking something that feels immediate, certain, and controllable. Emotional spending checks all three of these boxes.

It offers clear action with a predictable outcome. You click or pick up an item and throw it in your cart, swipe your credit or debit card (or even your phone these days) and you get an immediate increase in dopamine.

Immediate relief.

The world is uncertain. Today's world seems more uncertain than ever, even though every generation would likely experience the same type of uncertainty, but it's in the 'here and now' that matters most to every one of us, not what happened last year, last decade, or last century.

Having a sense of control becomes powerful. It's almost like an aphrodisiac.

Every time you spend based on emotion, your brain is remembering that sense of relief. What it calculated would bring you relief is reinforced when you feel relief.

The next time stress overwhelms you or even just shows up a little bit, you have that desire buy something. Your brain is reinforcing the solution.

Emotional spending isn't about being smart or stupid, weak or strong; it is simply about **learning**.

THE EMOTIONAL LAYER THAT MAKES THINGS WORSE

I don't know for certain, but I can reasonably assume that you feel as though damage is caused by the spending itself.

There can certainly be harm that comes from emotional spending. That harm is usually in the form of more debt, less money to pay current bills, and eventually perhaps relationship harm if you're married, in a long-term relationship with somebody who is counting on you financially, and so forth.

But the *real* damage isn't in the spending itself (unless, of course, we're talking about a massive spending habit that is completely obliterating your ability to survive financially).

The real damage comes from the regret we feel afterwards. You start thinking you have no self-control, that you are terrible with money, or that you can't be trusted.

The ironic part of all this is when you feel stressed over this purchase, it actually increases the likelihood you may make another emotional purchase in the future to deal with that stress, which only compounds the problem and we end up in a death spiral.

Eventually, all the person who's stuck in the cycle wants to do is get … *relief.* And the only way they see or have seen that they can get relief is through … *more emotional spending.*

So, they get more credit cards, or start stealing, or stop paying bills they used to pay regularly just so they can continue getting that emotional boost.

EMOTIONAL SPENDING IS NOT THE SAME AS CARELESSNESS

It's critical that we make this distinction.

When you are being careless, it implies indifference. It means you don't really care one way or another.

Emotional spending is rooted in exactly the opposite. You *want* to do the right thing, but you don't have the bandwidth. You *want* to do the right thing, but you're overwhelmed with a host of other responsibilities and simply need some short-term relief so you can deal with those other responsibilities. You *want* to do the right thing, but you are carrying too much weight in your life now.

Emotional spending is often a response to unmet needs[30]. When money becomes one of the few available pressure-release valves, it's going to be used that way.

As with any mechanical system that induces pressure, it needs a pressure-relief valve so the entire system doesn't explode.

As humans, we need pressure-relief valves, too, and many people find that pressure-relief through emotional spending.

30 Joyce Marter, LCPC. The Psychology of Emotional Spending (Psychology Today). May 12, 2023. https://www.psychologytoday.com/us/blog/mental-wealth/202305/the-psychology-of-emotional-spending#:~:text=Emotional%20spending%20is%20when%20someone%20spends%20money,*%20Make%20better%2Dinformed%20decisions%20about%20your%20money

THE HIDDEN NEEDS BEHIND THE PURCHASE

When you look more closely at this issue, you will find that emotional spending clusters around a few core needs. These needs are:

- Relief
- Identity
- Belonging
- Control

As it pertains to **relief**, that means we tend to emotionally find something that's going to make our day feel a little easier, the pressure a little less, and the anxiety a little softer. Emotional spending for relief is probably the most common thing that we deal with for those of us who actually care about our finances, but have struggled to get a handle on them, especially during difficult times.

As it pertains to **identity**, emotional spending would reinforce the person you want to be. This is incredibly common in many regions around the world. We are chasing a perception about how the "successful" person is supposed to look like, based on the size of their house or apartment, the type of furniture, brand of clothing they wear, or type of car they drive. For somebody focused on identity, they will constantly be chasing a new standard every few years. That's exhausting.

As it pertains to **belonging**, we are humans and by nature we crave community. We want to feel as though we belong. Emotional spending that helps us gain that sense of belonging is a powerful motivator.

As it pertains to **control**, people will emotionally spend when they feel as though other aspects of their life (or every other aspect of life) is completely out of control.

When you see these patterns regarding emotional spending, then the behavior you have taken on in the past starts to make sense. When it finally makes sense, then you can manage it yourself.

You can finally change that behavior because you understand where the motivation comes from and Serenity Aligned™ (see back of book) offers clarity when you might need it.

WHY RESTRICTION USUALLY FAILS

For the most part, when you're seeking to gain control of your financial life, to change the habits and patterns you've fallen into, the bulk of advice out there would have you tightening rules surrounding emotional spending.

They will tell you things like:

- No more discretionary spending!
- No more "treats!"
- No more room for error!

Unfortunately, even though this sounds reasonable on the surface, it often backfires. That's because restriction only increases pressure and, as we've seen repeatedly now, pressure leads to stress which leads to your brain desiring immediate relief, thus compounding the problem.

When pressure increases emotional load, the desire or need for relief only increases more.

When you set these kinds of hard, fast rules for yourself based on that type of advice, eventually the rule is going to crack and break. This is why so many people who get into these programs and follow this advice tend to fall into the habit of spending *even more intensely* when those rules break.

It's the same core reason why people who go on fad diets do well for a while, but when they slip, they end up putting on *even more* weight than they had originally.

When those strict rules crater, you risk getting into a much bigger financial hole.

AWARENESS CHANGES BEHAVIOR MORE RELIABLY THAN CONTROL

We're about to turn the page (literally and figuratively) to the next part of this book, the part where we can finally enact change that is going to last.

In order to do that, we have to fully accept and embrace that changing behavior is going to be far more effective than trying to grab control over some aspect of your life that you feel you have lost control of.

When you pause long enough to ask yourself why you want something, why do you really need to make this purchase, you interrupt the automatic loop your brain has created.

It's not about beating yourself up over a future purchase. It's not about talking yourself out of an emotional spend.

It's about **noticing** behavior and **pausing** it.

You can't do that if you're not aware. Awareness creates space and having that space gives you options your brain wasn't giving you in the past. Aarav The Serenity Genie™ is a powerful tool to help you gain a moment and improve awareness.

You need to understand and accept that there will be times during this process when you still choose to spend. That's okay. We're seeking progress right now, not perfection.

However, there are going to be other times when you realize what you actually need isn't the purchase at all, but relief from the stress you're enduring.

And there are many alternative, healthier ways to get that much-needed relief.

PERSONAL ACTION STEP 9: FEELINGS

The next time you feel the urge to spend because you're overwhelmed with stress and anxiety, I want you to ask yourself one simple question:

"What am I really trying to feel right now?"

That's it.

That's all you have to do for this action step.

You don't need to fix the feeling. You don't need to deny the purchase. Not yet. You don't need to justify anything, to me, to yourself, or to anyone else.

Just name the need.

The Serenity Aligned™ (see back of book) app has a section where you can simply make and track these notes. This is a wonderful way for you to keep track of these revelations and remind yourself when you're feeling stressed and want to purchase something that there ***is*** an underlying need not being met.

- Is it seeking relief?
- Is it seeking comfort?
- Is it seeking identity?
- Is it seeking control?
- Is it seeking rest?

Once the need is named, you're no longer operating on autopilot. You've flipped the switch and are now putting control within your grasp.

Over time, awareness will make it possible for you to expand your options.

You may find, for example, that your emotional spending tends to follow exhaustion. So, instead of going shopping when you're physically or emotionally drained, get some rest first.

Or you might discover that emotional spending follows loneliness. Next time, call a friend, family member, or somebody you love to talk to before you go out.

It may even follow stress, so reducing pressure somewhere else might matter more to your financial health and well-being than tracking for money flow better.

Money can still be part of the solution — but it doesn't have to carry the entire emotional load.

Use the daily missions in the app that take less than 5 minutes and it matters.

WHAT THIS CHAPTER IS NOT SAYING

This chapter is not, in any way, shape, or form, suggesting that all emotional spending is harmless or that limits don't matter.

They absolutely do.

But limits work best when they are shared with understanding. They aren't going to work that well when they're used as some form of punishment.

You can care about your future financial health without being cruel to your present self.

I want you to stop treating emotional spending as some type of moral failure. When you can do that, an important shift takes place.

- You become more honest.
- You become more curious.
- You become less reactive.

As we move through the process, hard and fixed behaviors begin to soften. They soften not because we are forcing change, but because you are understanding yourself better, understanding what motivates you and your actions, and what triggers your actions.

We're about to move from individual behavior to the structure of financial advice itself. Through this process we're going to explore why so many people feel behind before they have a chance to stabilize.

For now, it's enough to remember that you are not broken for wanting relief. You are not foolish for using what's available to you. And you don't need harder rules to change; you need clear signals with a kinder system to guide you.

And real progress has already begun.

Part Three

Stability Before Wealth

CHAPTER 9

Why Most Advice Starts too Late

Most financial advice starts where your life hasn't... yet.

— — —

Jake and Martha had been married for 12 years. They had one daughter. Jake held a blue-collar job and Martha worked at a local retail shop part-time while their daughter Melanie was at school.

They always wanted to own a home, but had never managed to save enough money for a down payment, and with Melanie getting older and the cost of food, clothes, and other necessities rising, they weren't sure they'd ever get 'ahead.'

That's the advice they heard from so many about achieving their dreams: *you have to save.*

They were only scraping by in life. Well, it didn't always *feel* like they were 'scraping by,' but with barely $500 in savings on average, they kept spending just about everything they earned on their basic necessities: food, rent, clothing.

Where they lived, rents soared after a major global event, and that put a stopper in any hope of saving more, even when Jake took some extra hours whenever they were available, which wasn't often.

Even Martha's hours were hit or miss. One week she'd get 20 or more hours. The next she might be lucky to scrounge up 10 hours for her employer.

One afternoon while browsing a local bookstore for a school assignment for Melanie, Martha found a 'New York Times Bestselling' financial book. She recognized the author's name but knew little about him. It cost a fair amount for their limited resources, but it promised tools and spreadsheets and workbook-style exercises to help them achieve their dream. But what it promised most was financial peace and wealth.

She bought it and began reading. It contained chapter after chapter of advice and most of it *seemed* (or felt) like common sense. Some of the later chapters were loaded with rich investment advice, sound commentaries about owning real estate, and even clever strategies to break into investing.

While she was excited about what she would learn from this book at first (and Jake certainly was, too, though he didn't have a mind for math or investments, he knew she could figure it out), Martha began to doubt that anything written on those pages was actually going to benefit them.

By the second half of the book, even though she'd been doing the exercises and diligently working on their financial system with the provided spreadsheets, she started to think, *'This isn't written for us.'*

The advice was solid. It made sense. Things like:

'Save now'

'Invest early'

'Take advantage of tax breaks and tax accounts'

'Let compounding interest accounts do the heavy lifting'

Yes, it was sound advice, but Martha began to feel like so many of us do when reading that type of advice:

This wasn't written for me.

Millions upon millions of financially struggling people the world over desperately grab onto highly marketed books and strategies and programs and courses and so forth, spending gobs of money they *know* they don't really have to learn from so-called 'masters' only to discover as they go through the material that it doesn't ***speak to them***.

It's not that the advice is wrong.

The problem is that there is one massive, glaring assumption that tends to be baked right into the background of the content and that is this:

It all assumes the person is already economically stable.

It assumes you have a consistent and predictable income. It assumes that after all your expenses, you have something left over at the end of each month. And it assumes that everything in your life is stable, that you're not constantly bracing for the next surprise.

What surprise could be coming around the next corner of your life? Oh, I don't know, perhaps your transportation breaks down, you have a health crisis, the heating system in your house fails, war breaks out, or energy costs jump suddenly.

For most people, there's *always* an unexpected expense lurking around the corner. And for most of us, that means we're constantly chasing our proverbial tails to pay for it, often taking out a loan or slamming ourselves with other debts, even borrowing from family or friends when desperate, which will take weeks or months or years (again) to pay off, just so we can start the process all over.

Having stability in life is not realistic for most of the world. We live in reality and while we may do 'okay' for a while (financially), there comes a time when we struggle.

So, when we turn to this constant flood of regurgitated financial advice that has massive, highly experienced marketing teams behind them, that advice can feel more like accusations than guidance.

- *Why aren't you saving?*
- *You should have been investing 20 years ago!*
- *What's wrong with you?*

Enough is enough. That's why this book came into existence… to serve the people -you, me, and hundreds of millions of others around the world- who do the best we can and still find it difficult to gain true, lasting financial peace.

THE SUBTLE MESSAGE BEHIND "GOOD" ADVICE

I'm not intending to mock or ridicule other financial experts or books or courses or counsel. No, they are sound and many of them sincerely desire to help people… and do.

However, there has grown a widening chasm between the men and women who give their advice and thoughts and experiences and the rest of us who live in the real world of struggle, who -no matter what we do- still live paycheck to paycheck.

All that other advice assumes we should be past the hard part already. Or that getting past the hard part is really simple, basic stuff, like: pay your bills, save, get a nest egg.

Yeah, easier said than done, especially in our modern global economy and shifting employment landscapes.

That's why, if you're not investing yet, don't have much money saved yet, it's easy to think you're behind. And for those of us in our 40s or 50s or 60s, that feeling of being behind can be crippling.

We start to think we missed every and any window of opportunity to be financially free.

It's as though we failed some invisible test of adulthood and now we'll have to pay for that the rest of our life.

But I want to say: **you didn't fail.**

You didn't fail any test.

You just never quite reached the starting line that all this other advice incorrectly ***assumes*** you're at.

STABILITY IS THE STEP EVERYONE SKIPS TALKING ABOUT

When you start reaching out for advice, you'll discover there are innumerable resources. Online, in books, through conferences and seminars, through local government and private programs, just to reference a few.

Many people begin looking for this information while dealing with crisis. Many start once they've finally managed to get out of the crisis because they wonder if there's a way *they* could possibly avoid slipping back down into that mess in the future.

If you're in crisis, sound financial advice will help. There are plenty of resources available with great tips and strategies.

If you've got a solid savings account or cash set aside, you'll find wonderful investment tips and strategies to help you build your wealth.

That's all wonderful.

However, there's a massive gap that exists between crisis and comfort.

This stage of financial life sits smack dab in the middle. It comes *after* survival but before growth.

This is the stage where income exists, but it fluctuates. Bills are getting paid (mostly), but the margins at the end of the month are thin (sometimes **razor** thin). One unexpected expense can undo months of solid savings effort. And planning feels too risky because the present isn't secure.

This is the **STABILITY GAP**. And this is where millions upon millions of people live.

Too often, financial institutions and their advice completely skips this stage. They jump from "get out of the crisis" to "build wealth!"

Sadly, instability changes everything.

You may have some people who got out of their crisis and even started investing thanks to that advice, but when instability creeps in again, when another crisis hits, they risk picking up old habits, which are rooted in stress.

That's why, even though you hear some amazing, wonderful stories of success these gurus talk about, you just don't hear of the more common tales of slipping and falling back into debt so many other people experience.

To properly move forward, we must first deal with this instability stage.

WHY ADVICE SKIPS THIS STAGE

I know there are probably several reasons (or excuses) why so much of the advice out there skips this stage. The cynic in me would want to say it's because there's no real money to be made in helping people get 'stable' financially.

But in reality, it likely has more to do with the fact that getting to a stable footing (not wealthy, mind you, but stable) doesn't provide the kind of awe-inspiring stories that increased wealth does.

It's not easy to sell this kind of stable middle ground, even though that's exactly where most of us sit... in the middle.

Another reason why so much of the financial advice you read or hear about skips this area is because the authors of those books and courses and seminars already passed through that stage a long time ago. Sure, it might have been during different conditions, but when we go through challenges and years pass, it's easy to forget just how difficult it was.

We tend to alter our perceptions of emotions over time (unless you keep a diary detailing exactly how you were feeling), so you can then look back and think, 'It wasn't as bad as I remember.'

Yeah, it probably was, but by the time people give advice, they forget how alone they felt, how lost they were. How far they truly were from serenity.

Also, we can't overlook the reality that there is a very real bias our culture tends to place toward optimization. Stability feels like standing still.

And people don't want to stand still.

They *crave* forward momentum.

They *crave* growth.

And that's where the bulk of financial advice sits in this world.

That's what we're aiming to change.

THE EMOTIONAL COST OF STARTING TOO LATE

Okay, okay, let's get down to the heart of this chapter.

When advice you're receiving assumes you already have stability, even when you don't, it creates a particular kind of anxiety.

It creates the kind of anxiety from which you will eventually feel like there's no real escape. No matter what you do then, you'll feel *more* trapped. Then you'll truly give up.

Why? Because you will feel pressured to think long-term when you're still straining under the weight of the short-term issues. The short-term volatility will continue to override your thinking and emotions.

You are told to focus on the future when the present requires constant attention.

Instead of creating consistency (as that advice predominantly focuses on), it will create paralysis.

Eventually (and, often, quite quickly), you'll start thinking:

- *What's the point of starting small?*
- *I'll wait until things get better.*
- *I should be further along than this.*

As enough time passes and you keep waiting for the right time to start, that waiting becomes avoidance.

You don't engage because you feel like if you *did* engage, it would be an admittance that you're actually behind.

And if so, **so what**?

I don't care if you're 20, 40, 60, or 80! If you're behind, guess what?

You're not that different from the rest of us.

You're not that far off from stability.

Once you gain stability, you can start building toward what you long for.

And yes, I honestly believe 80 isn't too late, either. But think about this: where you *will* be in 5 years won't be where you would have been if you had started 10 years ago.

But, then again, where you *will* be in 5 years won't be as great if you wait four years to start.

Wishes for what **could have been** are as useless as trying to regain a breath that's already left your body. You can't get it back, but here's the thing: that last breath was important, but not nearly as important as **the next one**!

Stability, my friends, is ***not*** a consolation prize. Not even close. It's **GROUNDWORK**!

Look at that word. Study it. Embrace it.

Groundwork.

Stability will allow:

- *Patience to exist*
- *Long-term thinking to feel safe*
- *Habits to take root*
- *Growth to be sustainable*

Without stability, every plan will feel fragile. Every setback you experience will feel catastrophic. Every piece of advice will feel like pressure instead of possibility.

So, let's choose stability first. This isn't lowering goals.

It's selecting the right order or things!

WHAT STABILITY ACTUALLY MEANS

When I'm talking about stability, I'm not talking about perfection.

There's no such thing as being perfect. In anything.

What I'm talking about regarding stability is having fewer surprises, more predictability, quicker recovery when something goes wrong, and less emotional whiplash.

Notice I didn't say *no* surprises. Financial surprises are *always* bound to happen. You can't avoid them. You can plan well, even exceptionally well, and still be surprised from time to time.

This level of stability is as much psychological as it is financial. You'll know that you're becoming more stable not when your net worth spikes, but when money takes up less mental space, when decisions feel calmer, and when you don't have to scrape by every month, worried about every penny.

When you don't have stability in your financial life, saving or investing can feel abstract. It might even feel threatening, believe it or not.

This type of financial advice asks you to commit money you might need for basic living expenses. It also asks you to trust systems that you don't have any reason to trust yet.

WHAT IT MEANS TO 'BEGIN'

We're going to **begin** now. This doesn't mean you have to jump into 'growth.'

We're not there yet.

For most of us, real beginning is about smoothing out our cash flow, creating **small** buffers (breathing room), reducing volatility, and building systems that won't collapse under stress.

You'll discover that when you start here, it won't look like much from the outside, but we don't care about that. We're not trying to impress anyone.

Though it may not look like much from the outside, it's going to change how you *feel* (and how life feels) on the inside.

That's going to make everything else possible.

To get there, you have to reframe the questions you ask. Instead of asking something like, "Why haven't I started investing yet?" You should ask, "What would make my financial life feel more stable right now?"

The answer may not be a specific amount of money you have or a percentage of your net income you save, but rather *predictability.*

It might be a sense of some real **breathing room**.

Or fewer emergencies.

This is real progress!

ACTION STEP 10: STABILITY

Take a few minutes and think about what stability would *feel* like in your life right now.

I'm not talking about financial numbers or goals, but feelings.

- What would change from day to day?
- What would take up less mental space?
- What would feel easier or calmer in your life?

Write your answer down. If you use Serenity Aligned™ (see back of book) for these exercises, you'll be able to be reminded of this answer when you're moving through these processes and growing in your financial walk, and that's a great way to observe real progress being made. Remember, when you reach stability and move to the next stage of your financial life, you may look back at this moment and think, 'It wasn't as bad as I remember,' because your brain will alter memories of this, so write it down

for your future self. ____
____
____

WHERE DO WE GO FROM HERE?

Our goal is to build **stability** (if you couldn't guess). We're going to do that step-by-step.

We're going to operate on the assumption that you don't have any surplus and we're not going to be seeking perfection.

We'll talk about creating breathing room, redefining "enough," navigating inflation without panic, and building systems that respect real life.

You're not behind because you haven't started where the advice begins; you're right where the advice should have started.

And now, it finally does.

CHAPTER 10

Building Breathing Room Where There is None

Stability is the first real goal, not wealth.

— — —

IMAGINE STEPPING INTO YOUR OWN PERSONAL HORROR STORY. WHILE you may not enjoy the horror genre (movies or books or television programs), you undoubtedly have heard scary stories at one time or another in your life. Maybe from parents or an uncle or friends while growing up.

It doesn't even have to be a frightening story, but a tense thriller, something wound tight and dramatic.

But imagine, if you will, that you've stepped into an unfamiliar place. It could be a house or a rundown building. It's dark. There's no electricity. It's quiet.

It doesn't matter *why* you're there; you've been sent for whatever reason and you're answering the call.

The sun set and you've got a cell phone with the flashlight app loaded on it.

You step into the dark, ears straining to grab sound. Nothing. You know there's something inside you **must** get to, otherwise you can't leave.

What happens as you take one step after another into that house?

Most likely, you'll tense up, right?

You don't know what's lurking around the next corner, in the next room, in the basement or storage closet. Something inside is telling you to be cautious, and that's creating more tension in your mind.

Doesn't it kind of feel like that when you run out money for the week? Sure, you may have a few dollars in your wallet or purse or stuffed under your mattress or in a box at home, waiting for a 'rainy day,' and you won't touch it until or unless you absolutely have to.

The tension you feel in those moments isn't happening because you're out of money.

It's happening because you don't exactly know what's coming next.

Like characters in thrillers or horror movies who have no clue what's in the next room, you don't know what tomorrow (or even later today) will bring. And ***that's*** what keeps you up at night. ***That's*** what drives your anxiety and fears about money.

If the world is stable, predictable, you would have already found a way to take what you earn and make it last one paycheck to the next so you'd never worry about running out.

But the world *isn't* stable. Not even close!

There's *always* something waiting around the next corner, in the next room, in that basement of life that'll startle you. Maybe even make you scream.

- It could be a car repair bill.
- Maybe it's not being able to work due to an illness or injury.
- It might even be some sudden expense you didn't plan on (that your spouse or partner made without consulting you).

This is called **life**. It happens. And these unexpected things *will* happen time and time again.

Don't they always seem to happen when you can least afford them? Well, if you could afford them, there wouldn't be tension.

If you had **breathing room**, then you could eliminate the constant anxiety that something bad is lingering around in the next room of your life, tomorrow, next week, next month, just waiting to jump out at you.

You see, creating genuine, measurable breathing room –not wealth— is the first step toward financial steadiness.

THE REAL STRESS IS VOLATILITY

Why do we get stressed about money?

Believe it or not, most people tend to focus *on* the money, whether it's the money they *don't* have or the money they *need*.

But that's not where financial stress **really** comes from. Yes, it does relate to funds, but I'm making the claim that the bulk of this stress you feel comes from volatility[31].

31 Ways to navigate market volatility and financial stress (North American Company). Jan. 6, 2025. https://www.northamericancompany.com/plan-for-tomorrow/ways-to-navigate-market-volatility#:~:text=It%20can%20be%20completely%20normal,term%20financial%20goals%20at%20risk.

Volatility is rooted in unpredictability in the financial world. Maybe you've heard the term bandied about within investment advice or on financial news segments.

"The stock market is showing signs of volatility," meaning, it's up and down and *seemingly* unpredictable.

Many of you reading this book probably feel tense and anxious about money when:

- **Your income is irregular.** Maybe you have an hourly job and you're not getting the same number of hours to work each week. Or you're a contractor (freelancer, gig worker, etc.) and the amount of work you get fluctuates.
- **Your expenses drift** up and down without warning. Utility bills, energy costs, food prices can all seem to rise and fall out of our control, and within days of world crises that might drive markets. But there are plenty of other ways your expenses can rise and fall without warning.
- **Your (financial) obligations shift** faster than you can adjust your plans.

Even when the financial numbers are manageable, volatility is going to create stress and we now know how your brain reacts and responds to stress: it's going to seek the quickest way out (relief).

You start recalculating, you end up constantly estimating, and you're always anticipating.

That's a tough way to live. The mental effort just *imagining* that right now as I write this is exhausting! Keep that up long enough and you'll eventually feel as though your money situation requires **constant attention** simply to remain afloat.

WHY PREDICTABILITY FEELS LIKE RELIEF

Your brain –the human brain— was designed to look for patterns[32]. Patterns make it much easier to process information.

Just consider language. Whatever your native language is -English, Chinese, Arabic, Russian, etc.- when you read words, what are you doing? ***What*** is your ***brain*** doing?

Not reading. It's interpreting.

You may read words out loud or silently in your head, but that's only because it's how you were *taught* to read.

Your brain sees each word, several words together, or entire paragraphs as **symbols**[33].

Patterns.

To your brain, a word is a bunch of lines, regardless of language. And it means *nothing*. It only represents *something*. It is a symbol.

And when your brain works best, it's looking for patterns. If you want to read faster, stop silent reading in your head and simply see the word and recognize it for what it represents, then you'll begin stitching several words together as phrases, and that's how people become speed readers, more efficient readers.

By helping the brain see the patterns.

When the patterns are clear, the brain relaxes. It can anticipate outcomes. It can plan better. It can trust the environment or situation or

---

32 Alice Park. Your Brain Learns New Words by Seeing Them Not Hearing Them (Time). Mar. 24, 2015. https://time.com/3757022/learn-to-read-see-neuroscience/

33 Alice Park. Your Brain Learns New Words by Seeing Them Not Hearing Them (Time). Mar. 24, 2015. https://time.com/3757022/learn-to-read-see-neuroscience/

circumstances enough to focus on something else. It can be led to true serenity.

When patterns are unstable, the brain stays alert. Constantly on edge. It treats every decision as potentially significant.

This is why two financial situations with the same income can feel completely different.

You might have a person with a higher income, but more uncertainty dealing with constant stress and strain around their money and another person who earns a lot less, but who has a predictable system who is calmer, more poised, and more confident in their financial life.

Predictability doesn't eliminate stress entirely, but it reduces the *frequency* with which stress is triggered. That reduction matters more than you realize.

"MORE MONEY" ISN'T ALWAYS THE FIRST SOLUTION

I do not want you to misunderstand this. Yes, we're about to dive into building a buffer, which *may* require more money, but the **first solution** is ***NOT*** more money… it's structure.

When you're making more money but don't have structure, this could increase volatility and thus stress. More income might come from a second part-time job, irregular bonuses, fluctuating gig work, or even inconsistent payment schedules.

There are plenty of jobs out there that don't pay regularly. Farming, fishing, drilling, mining, etc. When people go where the work is, they don't always know when the paycheck will come in… or how much it will be worth.

Even bringing in more money could mean unpredictability remains, especially if spending increases along with it.

Why would spending increase? As we saw in Part I, it's a stress relief mechanism.

We need to first build structure so that *when* we start bringing in more money (or freeing up some money), we'll have stability.

Now, what does 'breathing room' actually look like for you? It's different for each of us. And it's not a set dollar amount.

What I want you to focus on is a feeling of margin, a feeling of being able to breathe, *even when* (not if) those unexpected events hit.

What you want from this breathing room is to feel that:

- Small surprises won't derail everything
- Decisions don't have to be rushed
- The next month doesn't feel like an unknown cliff (or like you're wandering into a strange house in the dark)

So, what could breathing room be?

- Having a small buffer in your account (perhaps $50, $200, or even $500 or more, depending on you, your location, your expenses, your income, where you live, etc.).
- Knowing **exactly** when your bills are due.
- Having a plan for those unpredictable expenses.

So, let's start dealing with this now. And don't overlook the power Serenity Aligned™ (see back of book) can bring to your life, especially when you utilize its companion, Aarav The Serenity Genie™.

PERSONAL ACTION STEP 11: EXPENSES

Look at your current expenses. These are the regular, recurring expenses you have each month.

Rent or mortgage, utilities, food, transportation, and more.

Track ***only*** what has deducted money from your wallet or bank account in the past three months that are *recurring* withdrawals in Serenity Aligned™ (see back of book). This is what you're going to write down. (We'll deal with the extraneous expenses later).

The app will provide a quick and easy method to track all this, so you can update these expenses as you build more stability and breathing room.

Try to place them in order of the payment date. For example:

- April 1: $1,540 – rent
- April 3: $145 – electric
- April 10: $100 – Cable and internet

Next, Serenity Aligned™ (see back of book) will **add up all those expenses** and divide the total by three (three months) for you, providing your average monthly expenses. This is what you have going out consistently.

Now, review every one of those expenses. Is there something you could cut out? Even for a while? Depending on where you live and what you have coming in, you might not think so.

That's okay. You might find *something* you can trim.

Do you have a cell phone? A smartphone? What's the monthly cost for your plan? Is there something more affordable?

For your food expenses, look at what you buy every week. Does it include snacks, junk food, alcoholic beverages, soda? Those aren't necessary (not to mention being unhealthy, which leads to greater health issues and subsequent expenses later on in the form of bills or missed time at work).

Forget the notion that you 'like' them. Do you need them right now? That's the question.

Is the $5 per day coffee at a local cafe necessary? Is that going to add to your stress?

Cut those expenses that you can from your regular spending and see how much you save each month.

This will be diverted to your safety net. This becomes **breathing room**.

THE HIDDEN POWER OF SMALL BUFFERS

A buffer is simply a small amount of money set aside to absorb everyday unpredictability.

This isn't about emergencies. This isn't about investments. It's only about **friction**.

That friction could be a late fee you didn't expect, a slightly higher electric or other utility bill, or a yearly subscription you neglected to cancel or forgot was coming out automatically still.

In your Personal Action Step earlier, you didn't have to deal with earning more money. You didn't have to deal with your extraneous purchases. You only dealt with your **recurring** expenses and if you're able to find something to trim out, that will give you some breathing room.

When you don't have breathing room, every small surprise becomes a disruption. But with a buffer, the same surprise becomes a minor inconvenience.

Even a modest buffer –$50 or $100— can dramatically reduce the number of moments where you feel forced to react quickly.

Now, keep in mind that the *longer* you focus on keeping your regular expenses trimmed, the more you'll save. Then you'll begin building more than just breathing room.

You'll be building emergency funds and then investment capital, and that's where you can finally grow forward.

STABILIZING CASH FLOW

If you have the same paycheck every week or month or regular period, then this section will be of no use to you.

But for those who deal with unstable paychecks or unpredictable income, let's talk.

Finding a way to stabilize your cash flow is another opportunity to create breathing room.

Even if you *do* receive a regular, consistent paycheck, you may find that it comes on different time schedules than your bills, and when you're stressed, that can create a host of issues as we discussed in Parts I and II of this book.

While I'm not going to tell you to find a different job, I will tell you to do what you can to ensure that your bills come due around the same time that you tend to get paid.

For example, if you get paid on the first and 15th of each month, call your debtors, utility company, and so forth and request to have your due dates coincide with those paydays.

You should also clearly separate fixed expenses (rent, utilities, etc.) with flexible ones (streaming services, dining out, etc.).

While you're not going to be increasing your income this way, it will offer better clarity, and better clarity reduces stress.

REDUCING FINANCIAL 'NOISE'

We often overlook just how many decisions there are about our money. We are bombarded with choices, bills, and opportunities.

Subscription services, payment methods, bank accounts, small recurring charges –each adds another layer of complexity.

And speaking of small recurring charges, do you know why so many stores have all those seemingly 'little' items by the checkout counters? Those are called 'impulse' items.

They seem small (in price), but if you add up all the times you've grabbed gum, a candy bar, some mints, a small pack of batteries, or anything else at the 'spur of the moment,' you'd likely be surprised how much money you've actually spent on them.

It's even worse today with the Internet and countless 'subscription-based' services, whether it's entertainment or educational or creative.

That's a lot more financial noise to deal with.

When there's so much noise, your brain has to constantly filter the information and that takes attention and energy. That's when mistakes happen.

Simplify your financial environment to reduce the load.

Consolidate accounts, cancel unused or unnecessary services, or even reduce the number of active payment channels (the number of payment cards) you use.

None of this is dramatic, but it will make your financial landscape easier to navigate.

WHY BREATHING ROOM COMES BEFORE OPTIMIZATION

Many financial systems jump immediately to optimization. They tell you to:

- 'invest more,'
- 'minimize expenses,'
- 'maximize your returns.'

Optimization is valuable, but *only* once stability exists.

I know you just worked on finding something to cut from your current regular expenses, but you also have the option to move a bill to a different date (closer to your payday), or simplifying how money flows between your accounts.

You don't have to do it all right now.

Just choose one.

Implement it.

Let it settle.

Then choose another. Aarav The Serenity Genie™ will walk with you as you practice this daily.

The more breathing room you create, the more comfortable you become. The more comfortable you become, the more relaxed your brain is. The more relaxed your brain is, the easier it is to deal with the unexpected.

This is the **true beginning of progress**.

As you can see, we're not trying to gain wealth overnight. There's no legitimate system in the world that can do that, though too many books and experts convince you through marketing that it's *possible*.

It's not.

What we're doing here is building a **foundation** upon which you can build and grow… with a stable, solid structure.

Take this advice. Work with it. Implement it.

Once you see how breathing room affects you and your money mindset, the door opens wider.

And the possibilities stretching out before you grow bigger.

CHAPTER 11

A New Definition of "Enough"

"Enough" is the line that finally lets you breathe.

THOMAS WAS JUST OUT OF HIGH SCHOOL AND STARTING AT A prestigious university in another country. A child of successful parents (both of whom were seasoned professionals), he had been driven at an early age to be successful, too.

He set goals, kept a daily journal to track his progress, and monitored the business world so he could adjust his plans and goals as needed.

In all aspects, Thomas was programmed to reach the pinnacle of whatever industry he dove into.

And he did.

He landed a stellar job right out of college, worked tirelessly, putting in 70 and even 80 hours a week or more for his employer, and quickly moved up the management ladder.

With each step up the rungs to the top, he received raises and bonuses and became wealthier every year.

By the time he was 45, Thomas was worth almost $3 million, earning $300,000 annually with just his base salary. For all intents and purposes, Thomas had plenty. Well more than enough.

Yet he was never satisfied. He wanted more. It grew into an obsession and he thought, *'If I'm earning the same as I was last year, I'm failing.'*

It sounds absurd for someone earning that much money and that level of wealth to think they're *still* not earning 'enough,' but it happens, not just to the uber-wealthy, but the poor and middle class as well.

That's because there's a subtle, soft, and quiet promise that tends to be stitched throughout much of the modern financial culture.

It says, "If you just keep going, if you save just a little more money each month, if you cut a few *more* expenses, if you invest a little more, push yourself a little harder now, eventually you'll reach a point where things *finally* feel secure."

It continues, "You'll *finally* have **enough**."

That would likely mean enough money, enough stability, and enough margin to *relax.*

The problem tends to be that most people never feel as though they actually get there.

They strive, they work hard, they trim their spending, build a savings account that could impress just about everyone they know, they see their incomes rise, their investments grow, and yet no matter what they do, that sense of being 'almost there' lingers.

You never seem to reach 'enough.'

That's because 'enough' is an abstract concept. It's a moving target. **Enough** for one person might start out as $5,000 in savings, 10 percent of their income being diverted to investment accounts, and being able to afford a house of their own. For someone else, that number could be $50,000 in savings, $250,000 in assets, $1 million in investments, a primary house and a vacation villa, and several fine automobiles. Still, for another, it could merely mean having enough to eat each day.

Enough is certainly in the eye of the beholder, but *even if* there's a person out there who writes down what 'enough' would be for them, and *even if* they manage to not alter that, ever, most of the rest of us mere mortals don't operate (or think) that way.

For us, what we once viewed as being (potentially) enough changes.

It shifts. It moves. Why does it move?

Because when income rises, when savings accounts blossom, when investments are real, when *things are going well,* expectations quietly rise, too. When you discover that you can achieve these goals, these levels, then you start to expect more from yourself.

When one goal has been achieved, we tend to create a new one, or we simply move the goalposts (so to speak). The target shifts. What had once felt generous suddenly feels ordinary.

People have a tendency to spend more when they earn more. You can simply look around you, no matter where you live, and see this in action.

A person living in a musty, moldy studio apartment with cockroaches and rats in the walls starts earning more money. They get a promotion and a solid raise. Then what happens? They start looking for a better place to live.

At the time they're in that first apartment, they probably think, *'I can't wait to get a full one-bedroom apartment in a nicer area.'* Then they work hard and get there. After that, they may get married, want kids, but even if they don't, after a couple of months or years in that new, 'better' apartment, they long for *more* space, a nicer area, better views, and so forth.

What had once been thought to be optimal eventually becomes a burden.

Remember in Part I of this book we talked about how the brain adapts? It seeks relief from perceived *threats*. Well, it's not just going to adapt to threats –real or perceived. It's going to adapt to changing circumstances as well.

The brain resets its baseline and starts measuring again. This is called neuroplasticity[34]. So, if your sense of what will be 'enough' is based entirely on external benchmarks, it will keep moving indefinitely.

And yes, you, too, could become just like Thomas, earning more money than you'd be able to realistically spend in your life and still feel like it's never enough.

THE DEPRIVATION AND REBOUND PROBLEM

One of the most common pieces of advice when dealing with financial stress is to cut spending dramatically.

Yes, I had you look to try and trim some of your regular expenses, but what I'm talking about is the drastic tightening of spending right out of the gate.

Like a closeout sale, 'Everything must go!'

34 The power of neuroplasticity: How your brain adapts and grows as you age (Mayo Clinic). Apr. 12, 2024. https://mcpress.mayoclinic.org/healthy-aging/the-power-of-neuroplasticity-how-your-brain-adapts-and-grows-as-you-age/#:~:text=%E2%80%9CThe%20ability%20of%20the%20brain,to%20optimize%20your%20brain's%20potential.

At first, you'll feel scared, and once you do it, once you cut all subscriptions, stop eating out entirely, and eliminate every small pleasure from your spending patterns, it feels empowering.

It provides a sense of control. It shows that you can commit and follow through.

However, as time marches on, something changes. Life starts to feel smaller. Every single decision you make becomes a calculation.

Given enough time, you'll find that every purchase that used to feel 'normal' then carries emotional weight. Even when you go out to enjoy an evening with your spouse, partner, or friend, you will feel suspicious. "Why am I doing this?" You may think.

The strain will only grow. And the system you build on deprivation will also become strained.

That's not because discipline is wrong. It's not. It's a good thing. It's because discipline *without relief* leads to deprivation and that isn't going to produce long-term, lasting fruit.

Eventually, when you operate on a deprivation system, you'll end up with the **rebound problem**.

I've mentioned diet fads. While obesity may not be a serious problem in many parts of the world, in the U.S., it has become an epidemic. And though you may not be seeing or dealing with this in your neck of the world, simply understand that there are constant diet plans, fads, and programs that are developed and released every single year, marketed to a population that continues to get fatter every year.

Millions of people buy fitness programs, pills, and supplements, desperate for a shortcut to losing weight and feeling better physically.

Some percentage find success. They dive into the plans, lose weight, and look and feel better. Then what happens? They experience what psychologists call the *rebound behavior*[35].

Pressure they've put on themselves to lose weight grows until something inside breaks (inside their psyche, not literally something breaking in their physical body).

A stressful week might lead to grabbing their favorite chocolate bar or they get so hungry and spot their favorite snack or after months of deprivation, they splurge.

Before long, the weight is piling back on and that person starts to cycle into the familiar feelings of guilt, frustration, and failure.

If we're building our financial future entirely on restriction and deprivation, there's going to be a huge problem when it makes contact with real life.

THE EMOTIONAL PURPOSE OF SPENDING

Not all spending is the same. Some spending actually improves quality of life[36]. You've probably already experienced how some things you buy reduce stress (and I'm not talking about the immediate sense of relief your brain gets from that dopamine hit). Other purchases might save you time, making your life a little easier. And some purchases help to create meaningful experiences.

35 Iijima and Tanno. The rebound effect in the unsuccessful suppression of worrisome thoughts (Science Direct). March 23, 2012. https://www.sciencedirect.com/science/article/abs/pii/S0191886912001407

36 How purposeful spending contributes to long-term happiness (The Currency). August 1, 2023. https://www.empower.com/the-currency/life/purposeful-spending-experiences-over-things#:~:text=Even%20with%20the%20pinch%20of,feel%20better%20about%20their%20spending.

The problem is that so much financial advice that's on the market today doesn't differentiate between these positive purchases and other discretionary spending that simply wastes money. It's an 'all-or-nothing,' blow up everything until nothing's left sum game.

Money isn't simply a tool for survival or accumulation; it's also a tool that can shape daily life[37].

When used thoughtfully, spending can create rest and opportunities to refresh and recharge yourself, support relationships, reduce friction in life, and reinforce values. These things still matter. If we ignore them, if we merely toss them into the same category as every non-discretionary topic, we end up burning down the forest and the fields of flowers with the rubbish we're trying to eliminate.

ENOUGH IS NOT JUST A NUMBER

For many people, when thinking about what would be 'enough' financially, it's just a number. This might mean it's a:

- Certain balance,
- Certain income level,
- Or certain milestone.

Shatter that thinking right now. Get rid of it.

Numbers alone rarely capture what people are actually *seeking*.

What are *you* truly *seeking* by reading this book, doing the action steps, and continuing on? To hit a certain figure in your bank account? To reach a specific income level?

Or are you *seeking* a different **experience of life**.

37 Eric Roberge. Money Is a Tool, So Stop Treating It as the Goal (Forbes). May 27, 2015, updated June 30, 2021. https://www.forbes.com/sites/ericroberge/2015/05/27/money-is-a-tool-so-stop-treating-it-as-the-goal/

Most of us, when tackling these challenges in life, often want:

- Fewer financial surprises,
- Less background anxiety,
- More freedom to say yes or no *intentionally*,
- Or the ability to enjoy what we have without constant calculation and feelings of guilt.

To achieve these kinds of outcomes, we need to focus on perception as well as the numbers when figuring out what will be 'enough.'

And you need to be able to **measure** 'enough,' so that it doesn't become a constantly moving target.

THE CULTURAL PRESSURE TO ALWAYS WANT MORE

We live in a cultural age where dissatisfaction is magnified, and for a reason. If companies (and their marketing teams) can convince you that you're unhappy, then they can also convince you that they have the answer to happiness.

We're bombarded by advertisements every single minute of each day. The average person is exposed to between 4,000 and 10,000 ads *each day*[38] (depending on where you live)!

38 Sheree Johnson. New Research Sheds Light on Daily Ad Exposures (SJ Insights). September 29, 2014. https://sjinsights.net/2014/09/29/new-research-sheds-light-on-daily-ad-exposures/#:~:text=Those%20higher%20numbers%20not%20only,an%20impression%20(engagement):%2012

EACH AND EVERY DAY!

Let that sink in for a moment.

"Come on," you might be saying, "that's ridiculous. I'm not seeing that many ads every day!"

Are you sure?

You ride a scooter or drive your car, ride the bus, the train, walk down the street... what are passing? Billboards, signs on bus stops, handmade signs stuck in the ground, trucks with slogans on them, and that's just a small part of the day.

Every time you pass a flyer taped to a window, stapled to a telephone pole or glued to a light post, every time you go online and see ads on almost every web page, popups, and more. When you watch TV or even streaming services.

Ads are *everywhere*, and they have inundated us all.

That's a ton of noise to be exposed to, and there's almost no escaping it. There's almost no way to decode the secret to serenity when you're constantly under assault from outside.

The financial industry is all-in on advertising overload, and through years of propaganda, they've convinced people around the world that there is always a:

- **Better** investment strategy
- **More** optimized money management tool
- **Higher** income target to reach for
- **Larger** version of success

Ambition can certainly be motivating, but it also creates a quiet dissatisfaction with the present. You've probably experienced that; you attain a higher income range and though you once thought that would be optimal, you're not satisfied.

That's because when we're overwhelmed by all of this advertising telling us *someone* is better off than us, that *someone* else has what we should have, it's almost impossible to not measure yourself (and your self-worth) against that impossible standard.

You end up chasing hypotheticals rather than realities. In that environment, 'enough' becomes almost impossible to recognize, much less actually measure.

That's why we need to redefine **progress** for ourselves. If 'more' is the only definition of progress, then financial life becomes an endless chase. And that, my friend, is *exhausting*.

But we can define progress differently. We can measure it as:

- Fewer moments of panic,
- Quicker recovery after setbacks,
- Less mental energy spent on money,
- The ability to enjoy small comforts without guilt.

You're not going to find these measurements of progress in most financial headlines, but these are the ones that matter most to regular, average, everyday people... like you and me.

They represent movement toward stability.

PERSONAL ACTION STEP 12: A PRESSURE AUDIT

One of the most useful exercises you can do when you start thinking about having 'enough' is to conduct a **pressure audit**.

Make two lists –side-by-side in the Serenity Aligned™ app (see back of book).

In the first column, note all the expenses you can think of that genuinely reduce stress or improve your *quality of life*.

This might include services that save you time, small comforts that make the tough days a little easier to bear, or things that strengthen your relationships.

In the second column, jot down the expenses that create pressure (or increase it in your life).

These might include recurring costs that you barely notice, especially if they are automatically deducted from your bank account, purchases that are driven by comparison, or commitments that feel more like obligations than something that offers real value.

Once you generate these two side-by-side lists, you'll see more clearly where pressure originates.

But keep in mind that we're not going to try eliminating everything from that second column right away. Often, just cutting a few high-pressure expenses offers more relief than eliminating small joys.

This entire process is streamlined in Serenity Aligned™ (see back of book). Then Aarav The Serenity Genie™, your personal companion will listen to these answers and be a calm voice of reason whenever you need it.

THE QUIET RELIEF OF ENOUGH

When your definition of enough grows clearer, something subtle happens: you stop chasing every opportunity for 'more.' You stop comparing every decision to someone else's life (or someone else's definition of 'good enough'). You start evaluating choices based on alignment rather than status.

'Enough' is a foundation, not a finish line. When you recognize the common problem 'enough' creates, you stop chasing after a never-ending moving target.

Financial advice today often assumes that the goal for people is constant ***expansion***. But it's not.

For most of us, it's peace of mind, consistency, and a life that feels balanced.

Once the proper foundation is laid, then every financial decision becomes easier.

In the next chapter, we're going to turn to one of the pressures that most frequently disrupts people's sense of enough: **inflation**.

And we'll dig into how to respond to rising costs without falling into panic or overcorrection.

Because, when you pause and think about 'enough,' what happens when inflation continues to climb? You'll *never* get to that goal.

CHAPTER 12

Inflation is a Fact of Life

Rising costs require calm, not panic.

— — —

IT DOESN'T MATTER WHERE YOU LIVE, *INFLATION* IS A PART OF LIFE. Always has been; always will be.

There are, in fact, several things that are a part of life, and too many people worry about the things we (they) cannot change or affect, inflation being one of them.

When you dig down to the core of financial stability and security, you would be hard-pressed to find something more disruptive (on a regular basis) to this sought-after sense of peace than inflation.

Most of us tend not to notice inflation when we're younger. Sure, you can probably recall a time when your favorite guilty pleasure purchase (a chocolate bar, for example) only cost X amount of money, something you probably could scrounge up from the couch cushions or scouring the ground for dropped change. But now it has more than doubled or tripled or quadrupled that price, and it's only been a decade or two since those fond memories.

Everyone can tell of the 'good ole days' when it comes to the cost of just about any item.

That's because, as you grow older and your responsibilities increase, you have no choice but to pay closer attention to these things. Yet, 'noticing' it happens slowly at first, not usually in one big 'Aha!' revelatory moment. (I'm talking about the general inching up of inflation, not the sudden spikes that catch everyone off guard).

Companies have become adept at disguising inflation, focusing on pushing desired items up first (when they have a choice). The highly desired items will still sell, and that includes not just guilty pleasures of life but also the absolute necessities. After those increased prices settle in, then they'll bring up other prices[39].

The cost of eggs and milk go up. Then bread. Then canned goods. It might be a small percentage, but you begin to notice that $100 of groceries that got you through two weeks with your family now costs $120 or $130.

Some items will fluctuate, up and down, but generally almost always tending up, like gasoline.

Even some bills start to feel heavier, and it digs into your paycheck a little harder and deeper. That's when most people start noticing inflation.

Yet, for many years, even though inflation will continue to bring up the cost of things, it's subtle. Sometimes you'll even assume it's temporary.

It's not.

39 Megan O'Brien. 8 Expert-Backed Strategies to Deal With Inflation at Your Business (Circular Edge). March 3, 2022. https://www.circularedge.com/blog/8-expert-backed-strategies-to-deal-with-inflation-at-your-business/#:~:text=For%20businesses%20that%20must%20raise,term%20losses%20in%20market%20share.

When these soft, subtle changes happen over time, if your income doesn't rise to meet those costs, eventually you will feel the pressure. Stress will mount.

As inflation continues to outpace your income levels, the stress will only grow deeper.

Then, when there's a sudden and significant spike with inflation, then everything gets tighter. Fast. This is often when the ground shifts beneath your feet. Your financial feet.

Think of it like an earthquake. Every day there are mild and minor quakes all around the world. Most of them are so deep or so minor that few people even notice them, but over time the pressure in those tectonic plates continues to build until one day there's a major earthquake where thousands or millions of people notice and feel it.

It's those larger quakes that cause real damage. Just like sudden large inflation leaps.

When they hit, the numbers you trusted no longer behave the same way. Your paychecks don't stretch as far. Any margin you had (or thought you had) suddenly vanishes and you have no breathing room and everything starts to fall apart.

This is what inflation does, not just to the economy, but to the psychology of money.

Yes, some of you *may* have struggled with your finances for your entire adult life. Some may have chased the wrong things and found yourself in debt just trying to keep up with the perception of success and happiness you saw with friends or family or neighbors or people you never met on social media.

However, for many people who struggle financially, it's not because of anything they did or didn't do; it's because inflation rose too sharply, for too long, and before you really understood how to navigate the shifting landscape, you slipped into survival mode, reinforcing behaviors and decisions you knew you shouldn't.

WHY RISING PRICES FEEL SO UNSETTLING

When the costs of everyday items (including necessities) climb, it creates a double-edged problem. First, you have to deal with the **actual** increase in prices. Second is the *perceived* issues for your future.

What I mean by this is that when inflation jumps, people tend to tighten their spending in response to less disposable income. ***Then*** they think about the future and look to their employer for a raise (or, for entrepreneurs and small business owners, they might raise prices), and in order for companies to meet this increased demand for higher wages, they raise the cost of their products and/or services to their customers, thus perpetuating the inflation pressures.

There's a distinct psychology surrounding inflation that helps to exacerbate it[40]. But we don't control how everyone else reacts, only how *we* react.

Inflation increases create uncertainty. As we've seen already, uncertainty creates stress and stress causes your brain to react in a more primal, immediate-need-for-relief manner, thus creating a more challenging situation to try and dig your way out of in the long run.

When prices change quickly and unexpectedly, the mental map about your financial world can no longer match reality. What you expected to cost a certain amount of money no longer aligns with its actual cost.

Your brain is suddenly forced into a state of trying to recalculate and recalculate and recalculate. Some of us start asking things like:

---

40 Dent and Crockett. Why Thinking About Inflation Leads to More Inflation. April 10, 2022 (The Hustle). https://thehustle.co/why-thinking-about-inflation-leads-to-more-inflation

- Can we still afford this?
- Should we start cutting back now?
- What if prices keep rising?

Others of us ignore the situation and instead decide to bury our head in the sand like an ostrich. We ignore the dwindling savings, the rising debt, and begin putting bills aside for "later," and 'later' comes even later and later each month.

Anxiety drifts in, causing our brain to seek relief, which drives us into the cycle we went over in Part I and II of this book.

When people feel financial uncertainty, they tend to respond with urgency. They make sudden changes.

- They might cut expenses aggressively.
- They may abandon routines that had brought comfort in the past.
- They might start making drastic adjustments to plans. (That vacation they had planned might get canceled, etc.)

These reactions *feel* responsible, and they are certainly about taking action, but this type of **urgency** can also create problems.

Large, reactive changes often introduce new instability, especially when they're made quickly and under emotional pressure[41].

When that happens, there's a kind of opposite reaction that follows. You will likely feel exhausted mentally and give in to impulse purchases and then get back to tightening. You end up in a dangerous cycle that creates emotional and mental and financial whiplash.

41 Gen Z in Crisis: Money, Mental Health, and the Fight for Stability (Arta Finance). December 18, 2024. https://artafinance.com/insights/gen-z-in-crisis-money-mental-health-and-the-fight-for-stability#whats-fueling-the-crisis

PANIC IS A POOR FINANCIAL STRATEGY

When you panic (financially) it probably *feels* productive. You think you're actually doing something positive for your financial health. It may even create intensity ("See how I'm getting ahead of this?")

Unfortunately, it narrows your thinking. When you panic (financially), you might:

- Focus only on **immediate** threats
- Ignore long-term consequences
- Make decisions that relieve anxiety quickly rather than *effectively.*

Financial systems work best when **they are calm enough to absorb change *gradually***. That's where true serenity comes in.

What Does Inflation Actually Change?

It's true that money won't go as far when inflation increases. The same dollar buys less over time. This affects savings, planning, and breathing room.

However, despite what you *think*, inflation doesn't erase stability (and **stability** is what we're working on developing).

A calm response will generally involve **gradual** adaptation. A calm response will adjust spending patterns, rebalance priorities, and make *small* structural changes over *time*.

The goal isn't to ignore inflation; it's to respond properly and proportionately.

Even when you're not thinking it, if your emotional response to inflation is panic, your brain starts compressing all those thoughts (about the rising costs of things) into one basic conclusion:

Everything is getting worse.

That's a trap. That level of thinking only increases stress and stress patterns. You know what happens then.

Financial reality is rarely that simple. Sometimes, yes, *many* things might increase at a breakneck pace. Most of the time, though, *some* items increase while others hold steady. Some of your spending categories will remain fixed... for years, even.

When you can step back and view the *entirety* of the financial landscape and not just *some* prices, then you'll be able to respond more strategically rather than just emotionally.

THE POWER OF INCREMENTAL ADJUSTMENT

One of the most effective (and positive) ways to deal with inflation – regardless of whether it's basic, 1 - 3% levels, or sudden and sharp (i.e. 6 - 12%)– is to focus on small, *deliberate* adjustments.

There are numerous ways we can do this, for example:

- Gradually shift a few spending categories,
- Revisit subscriptions or other recurring expenses you may not use often,
- Adjust your expectations for certain discretionary purchases.

None of these actions will feel dramatic. They shouldn't. If it's one thing we want to avoid, it's the *dramatic* shifts.

You want to keep your overall system intact and balanced, and by avoiding the dramatic, emotional panic-driven reactions, you can manage that.

By focus on smaller adjustments, we can also avoid the "reset" trap.

Have you ever done that? You:

- Create an entirely ***new*** financial outline.

- Impose strict rules where you never really had hard and fast rules.
- Try to overhaul every habit at once.

Sure, when the pressure (seems) on, this type of reset tends to collapse under real life. You've probably already discovered that setting difficult standards tends to cause that new plan or system or goal to fall apart when you meet with some resistance. Or when you miss the mark just once.

Like all those New Year's Resolutions you might have made in the past that never survived January (or whatever your first month of the year is).

Inflation drives us into new ***unpredictability***.

The desire to regain *some* predictability is natural, but focus on strengthening the structures you already have in place and that remain within your control. Even if you don't think you have any formal structure, it's there, unspoken and unwritten, for yourself and your family.

The best way to strengthen your structure is to:

- Review spending categories and patterns periodically rather and constantly.
- Set aside small buffers (breathing room) for the inevitable price fluctuations that *will* occur.
- Simplify financial systems so adjustments are easier.

You're not going to eliminate inflation with predictability within your financial system, but you can restore a sense that your finances are manageable, even *when* prices increase.

PERSONAL ACTION STEP 13: RISING COSTS

If you've been affected by inflation (now or in the past), this simple exercise can help you.

Choose one spending category that has increased ***noticeably*** over the past year. It could be groceries, transportation, or utilities.

Then answer the following questions:

1. Has my spending actually increased? Or does it only *feel* like it has?
2. If it *has* increased, what is the smallest adjustment that could offset part of that change?
3. What spending category matters less to me that could absorb some of this shift?

Serenity Aligned™ (see back of book) is ideal for entering your answers. You can then update or add new categories to this list over time. Then you'll be able to quickly and easily monitor the impact inflation had, has, and will have on your financial mindset moving well into the future.

Remember, you're not trying to solve *every thing* right now; you're merely redistributing pressure. Then Aarav The Serenity Genie™ will help you handle the future better when you use it consistently.

CALM IS THE COMPETITIVE ADVANTAGE

Calm decisions regarding financial systems will *always* outperform reactive decision-making. Every time.

If you can remain steady and calm during uncertain periods, you'll tend to make fewer mistakes. More importantly, your brain will have the time and space to process information to help you find the **best** solution for whatever circumstance you find yourself in.

Remaining calm doesn't mean you're ignoring reality; it means you're refusing to let fear dictate every response.

Inflation will rise or fall over time. You can't change it. Economic conditions will shift. Prices will change.

Stop trying to build a system that attempts to control it. You can't.

How people prepare for *and* respond when an earthquake finally strikes will determine their ability to survive and thrive. It's no different in the financial world.

When our responses are measured, flexible, and intentional, the financial system you built remains resilient, even during uncertain times.

As you move forward, focus on **small** changes, **incremental** changes.

When you do, you'll be in a great position to effectively adapt to external pressures and build practical tools to manage

everyday finances more effectively.

For now, remember:

Rising prices require adjustments

They don't require you to panic.

Calm adaptation is one of the most powerful financial skills you can build.

Part Four

Practical Money for Real Life

CHAPTER 13

Designing a System That Fits Your Life

“

A good financial system bends… so it doesn’t break.

———

When Mary was struggling, tightening her spending didn’t really make a difference. She had purchased a few books over the years on managing finances, digging out of debt, and even started a famous self-guided ‘financial course’ program (though she never came close to completing it).

The divorce and subsequent years struggling to make ends meet hit her hard. She crunched numbers plenty. She bought specially designed books set up to track every possible category of regular spending, including charitable donations and student loans.

She would figure out her average monthly income and spending, put everything into those columns and start with a sincere intention of following through.

And she would. For a while.

Then she'd miss a day, forget to enter her spending, and then fudge a few numbers when she *knew* she shouldn't have bought what she did.

When a few days slipped into a week, the financial system fell into disrepair. Before long, she essentially abandoned the whole thing and tried her best to forget another failed effort.

Maybe you're someone who's done something similar, even if you never bought a financial book or course or attended seminars before, you might have tried to financially cut your way out of financial stress and pain.

But it didn't work, and the thought of doing that again could make your head start to throb, your chest tighten, and sweat begin to form on your brow.

Few words in personal finance can trigger such resistance and anxiety as the word *"budget."*

For some, the term can bring forth memories of spreadsheets they abandoned after a few weeks. For others, they might think of a financial system that collapsed under the weight of daily life. And still others may recall rules that felt more like punishment than planning.

And still for others, the resistance is quieter. Softer. Gentler. But it's still there. Maybe you tried trimming your spending before (and probably several times, at least), and it may have worked fine for a while, but eventually its rigidity became too exhausting to maintain. Or inflation or some external change put too much strain on the system and you abandoned it.

It is one of the first and most common directives from almost every financial program, guide, or self-help book in the world. Yet, as we've seen by now, that wasn't the right starting point.

WHY SO MANY FINANCIAL SYSTEMS FAIL

The long and short of it is this: most traditional financial guidance systems tend to assume a level of *predictability* that real life rarely provides.

These systems assume that:

- Expenses stay consistent,
- Income arrives on schedule,
- Unexpected costs are rare,
- Emotional energy is always available for careful tracking.

If those four aspects hold true, then you're far more likely to develop a financial rhythm that fits your personal life, and one that you can stick with. But what happens when any kind of volatility enters the picture?

For example:

- **Expenses might fluctuate.** Just remember the last time the cost of food or energy (like gas) or utilities rose and you weren't expecting it.
- **Income varies.** Maybe your hours were cut during a slow season or you couldn't get a raise when inflation jumped.
- **Surprise expenses hit.** A child or you had an unexpected visit to the doctor or your home heating system failed.

Personal energy –as we've seen— is limited. You can only do so much each day, and you can only handle so much during challenging times.

When a financial system depends on precision in an *unpredictable* environment, that's when you're going to have trouble[42].

That's usually the time when your financial rhythm will break down.

42 Trina Paul. Here's Why Budgets Don't Work for a Lot of People (CNBC Select). Dec. 19, 2025). https://www.cnbc.com/select/why-budgets-dont-work-for-people/#:~:text=Budgeting%20is%20difficult%20when%20your,to%20stick%20to%20a%20budget.

Many of these systems fail not because they're too simple, but because they are built with an expectation of exactness. People try to assign every dollar of their income and spending to precise categories, and they track each purchase carefully, and end up creating a detailed financial system that's meant to capture every movement.

Sure, this feels wonderful at first. You might think, *"Yes! This is going to work!"* You start enthusiastically. It feels empowering.

You can feel as though you're *finally* gaining control over your financial health. But that precision will, over time, begin to feel like pressure instead.

As we've detailed so far, when you're under pressure, you're under stress and strain. And when you're under stress, your brain interprets that as a real and immediate threat to your life and seeks relief.

That's where the edges of your precise system begin to fray and then fall apart.

Because any *unplanned* expense disrupts the system. Eventually that feeling of being organized and empowered can morph into feeling monitored… by your own spreadsheets.

That's where friction comes from and friction (again, as we've seen) will cause even the best systems to unravel and/or be abandoned. That's why fewer than 25% of people who build a budget stick to it[43].

It's ironic when you think of it: the desire for *perfect control* tends to produce no control at all as you surrender to your brain's overriding survival principles.

---

43 Rajeev Dhir. How Many People Actually Stick to a Budget? The Answer Might Surprise You (Investopedia). Sept. 02, 2025. https://www.investopedia.com/how-many-people-actually-stick-to-a- budget-the-answer-might-surprise-you-11799284#:~:text=Less%20than%2025%25%20said%20they,how%20and%20whether%20people%20budget.

FLEXIBILITY IS NOT FAILURE

In my opinion, too *much* financial advice **fails** to allow flexibility into their systems.

You're told to develop structure, to cut every extraneous, unnecessary expense from your life, and do it perfectly (well, you're not *told* to do it perfectly, but it's *implied*).

But this is one of the most **important** shifts you can make in your financial thinking:

A financial system is not a rule book.
It's a guide.

Its purpose is not supposed to be about enforcing perfection. The purpose of doing all this is to help you see what's happening and adjust accordingly.

If a way of working with your money cannot tolerate real life, if it doesn't allow flexibility (i.e. Unexpected expenses, emotional spending, shifting priorities, etc.) then the system is flawed.

It will more often lead to failure, then feelings of guilt, and a return to harmful emotional spending (possibly even more harmful habits).

Your financial life is dynamic. Your system should be, too.

Let's take a few categories of most common traditional tools as an example.

When you may have worked on your finances in the past (if you haven't ever done this yet, just follow along with the concepts… they're pretty simple to understand), you probably had a few categories such as:

- $400 for groceries
- $150 for dining out
- $100 for entertainment
- $250 for gas (if you own a car and commute to work)

In theory, this kind of structure should encourage economic consistency and support.

But in reality, it invites tension into your life. When you spend more on groceries one month or if a social event comes up and you didn't have *anything* to account for that, or if fuel costs jumped for some reason?

You need to constantly make corrections, cuts elsewhere, and you suddenly feel as though you have no breathing room.

Rigid systems are born to fail.

Flexible systems provide the ability to maneuver through real life.

A RANGE-BASED APPROACH

One of the simplest ways to build a personal financial rhythm that accommodates real life is to think in terms of **ranges rather than fixed numbers**.

Instead of assigning a single limit, define three zones for certain spending categories. It might be:

- **Minimum:** the lowest realistic amount you might spend.
- **Target:** the *typical* amount you expect to spend.
- **Stretch:** the *upper* boundary that still feels manageable.

In our example from earlier, someone set $400 for their groceries. For a **flexible** system, you might set it up like this instead:

- **Minimum** for groceries: $400
- **Target** for groceries: $500
- **Stretch** for groceries: $600

This approach recognizes that real spending naturally fluctuates. Some months you'll land near the 'minimum' while other months will get closer to the 'stretch'.

Just think, if you need toilet paper or cooking oil one month that stretches your limits and can't push that expense down the road, it might very well cause you to blow past your fixed system. But with a flexible system, you have room for real life.

The range you create keeps fluctuations in spending within a healthy boundary. This will reduce the emotional pressure that comes from treating every variation as a mistake.

SEPARATING FIXED AND FLEXIBLE SPENDING

In just about every part of life there are fixed and flexible expenses.

Fixed expenses tend to be things like:

- Rent or mortgage
- Insurance
- Loan payments
- Recurring bills

Flexible expenses tend to be things like:

- Groceries
- Transportation
- Entertainment
- Discretionary purchases

When you end up treating these two types of spending the same, it causes confusion. It causes tension.

By separating them, you will bring clarity to your system and your life.

Fixed expenses show what *must* happen.

Flexible expenses show where *adjustment* is possible.

This distinction allows you to respond to changing circumstances without feeling like the entire system is collapsing.

SIMPLICITY MATTERS

When Mary built a budget, it was all-encompassing. I mean, it had every conceivable category included, and that meant categories she never even spent money on.

Still, she filled in the numbers.

When she would open that finance tracking book and fill in the expenses for each day, her eyes (and brain) were met with a plethora of data. And small numbers, since there's only so much space you have to work with on paper (or a screen), or difficult to track and maintain.

Because it was complicated, it required more energy to maintain and that led to failure.

The focus of a *good* financial system is to **reduce mental strain**, not compound it.

For you, this may mean tracking fewer categories, developing simpler tracking methods, or even less frequent monitoring. Instead of sitting down every day to enter your spending, do it once a week. Keep track of your spending somewhere simple, like an app on your phone so you don't forget. But only dig into this once a week.

You might only need to review your details once a week. Others may only need to do it once a month.

What matters is that the system is simple enough to fit into your natural life rather than constantly interrupting it.

Plus, I want you to keep something very important in mind when you do develop a financial system and rhythm for yourself:

Many people unconsciously treat their financial health like a report card. If they stay within their flow of money, it feels like success, but if they don't, it feels like failure. *They* feel like a failure. Most people will *not stick* with *any* system when it makes them feel like a failure. They'll abandon it and just 'deal with it,' whatever 'it' happens to be.

A financial approach or system is supposed to be a tool. Something to ***inform*** you. When spending shifts, that practice should provide feedback about what's happening. When you have feedback, you can adjust your plan rather than criticize yourself or feel guilty about it.

Think of this financial tool as a compass. Remember our example of sailing across the ocean? If you use a compass and a storm knocks you off course, you don't throw that compass overboard.

You use it to help you get back on track, back on the right course and heading.

Don't throw out your compass ***when*** you slip off course. Instead, use it like the navigation tool[44] it's meant to be.

When a money framework is working well, it produces a very specific feeling: Calmness.

You have a general idea about where your money is going, you know how much flexibility you have, and when surprises appear, they require adjustment, but don't create panic.

When this happens, decisions become easier because the boundaries are clear without being rigid.

When you have a sense of calm connected to your finances (or because of it), that's a good sign that it's aligned with *reality*.

When Mary finally discovered the right system, it changed everything for her. She was able to celebrate the small victories, recover from the missteps, and even have more time to spend with her two boys.

---

44 Budgeting: It's GPS for Your Money (Boston University). https://dfr.oregon.gov/financial/manage/pages/budget.aspx#:~:text=Budgeting%20helps%20to:,of%20money%20during%20the%20month

One simple move can change everything for the better.

PERSONAL ACTION STEP 14: GENTLE FINANCIAL RHYTHM

If your current approach feels overwhelming or you've been avoiding looking at your spending and income altogether, start with a simple exercise.

Divide your spending into just three *broad* categories:

1. **Essentials**
   This would be things like **housing, utilities, transportation,** and other obligations.
2. **Living Expenses**
   That would be **groceries, everyday purchases,** and routine spending.
3. **Flex Spending**
   This would include things like **dining out, entertainment, hobbies,** and other discretionary choices.

I want you to **track these categories for <u>one month</u>** using Serenity Aligned™ (see back of book).

Don't aim for perfection. Don't try to make adjustments. Just ***observe***.

This exercise is only designed to build *awareness* without the pressure commonly connected with other tools that quietly demand perfection.

Once you do this for a month, you will be able (and ready) to gradually refine the system in ways that feel useful rather than burdensome.

PROGRESS OVER PRECISION

I know I've repeated the slogan, **"Progress, not perfection"** a couple of times in this book because it's vital.

But you can also say, **"Progress over precision."**

A financial tool doesn't need to be perfect to be effective. It just needs to be clear enough to *guide* decisions and *flexible* enough to survive **real life** (because that's where most of us live).

When behavioral awareness respects real life, when it allows for variation, acknowledges uncertainty, and prioritizes clarity over perfection, it becomes something actually useful for the rest of us mere mortals.

That kind of financial system becomes ***supportive***. And support is what most people have been missing with those other financial books and programs and courses.

In the next chapter, we're going to look at debt from a different perspective, from one that removes the guilt often attached to it while still offering a clear path toward progress.

For now, though, remember that a good way of working with your money does not demand perfection. It should simply help you see where you are so you can move forward with ***confidence***.

CHAPTER 14

Debt Without the Guilt

Debt is not your identity;
it's something you can navigate.

— — —

Debt doesn't *always* produce guilt. But, often, it does. Even if you don't *feel* guilty because of the debt you carry doesn't mean it's not nagging at you subconsciously.

Debt is basically something you *owe* for something you have already received. It's an **imbalance** in your life.

And while debt in our modern age has become synonymous with living life, it wasn't always the case. For most of history, people generally had to live within their means. They had to have money to buy things, whether that was food or shelter or jewelry.

Throughout history, people have been able to borrow resources to attain things they needed in the moment, and just like today, a person's ability to repay that loan (as well as how well respected he or she was in society) generally determined whether they received the needed funds.

Yet, we've never seen the level of debt or the accessibility of easy loans as we've witnessed in the past couple of decades ever before in history.

Using credit cards, loans to go on vacation, loans for home improvement projects, and so on have skyrocketed at a breakneck pace. While ballooning debt may be more of a problem in the U.S. and some European nations, almost every corner of the world has populations that turn to borrowing to 'get ahead,' or 'get relief' from the daily pressures of life, so it's a vital topic to discuss.

In the U.S., for example, household debt increased 5.5% in the final quarter of 2025[45]. Total household debt in the U.S. now sits at $18.8 *trillion.*

Most of us can't even fathom that level of debt. If my math is correct, with about 330 million Americans, that equals $57,000 in debt *per* U.S. citizen. That average includes babies and children and teenagers who never took loans or borrowed money, meaning the actual amount owed by average adults is much, much higher.

Do most of these people feel guilty over their debt? From the numbers, it may be easy to assume 'no, they don't.' But is that true?

45 Adriana Ocanas. Household Debt at New High, According to Latest Fed Report (US News). Feb. 11, 2026. https://money.usnews.com/credit-cards/articles/household-debt-at-new-high-according-to-latest-fed-report

The emotional weight of debt for many of us can be brutally heavy[46]. Debt can reshape how people see themselves. We've gone over some aspects of this earlier.

You might think:

- *I should have known better.*
- *I shouldn't be in this position.*
- *I'm never going to catch up!*

It doesn't matter if you've never spoken those kinds of statements out loud or even mentally considered them; the notion behind them may very well linger in the background of your life. And those notions, that sense that something is not aligned properly in your financial life can begin influencing how you approach spending and your finances.

Debt becomes more than just a financial obligation. It becomes its own story. It's a story that you may not be able to sit through, or want to.

THE MORAL LANGUAGE SURROUNDING DEBT

One of the reasons why debt feels so heavy in our lives is because of the language that surrounds it. Debt is often framed in our culture through a moral lens.

People are told they're irresponsible if they have too much debt or if they depend on debt to make ends meet.

They're told that if they need to borrow then it reflects a lack of discipline.

They're admonished to eliminate debt as quickly as possible, otherwise they should be ashamed of it.

46 The Psychology of Debt (Homewood Health Centre). https://homewoodhealth-centre.com/articles/the-psychology-of-debt/#:~:text=Debt%20can%20have%20a%20significant,insecure%2C%20inadequate%2C%20and%20helpless.

Yes, sometimes urgency can motivate action, but that's rarely going to lead to long-term benefits. It's more like trying to apply a Band-Aid to a gaping wound. You still have to apply pressure, and while it may slow the bleeding, you aren't going to heal anyone.

When debt becomes a moral failure (it's not, in most cases, but the *language* we use to describe it or to describe how we use it and treat it can make it feel that way), looking at your debt will be painful.

Most of us are programmed to want to look *away* from things that are painful.

Just think about the last time you suffered a serious injury (if ever). You felt the pain in your shin or arm or ankle, and whether there was a cut or broken bone or other obvious injury, if you looked at it, what would happen? Your eyes would exacerbate the pain, wouldn't they?

There's a reason we tend to look away from injuries to ourselves or others: our brain can interpret the scene and we *feel* the pain, too.

Within our financial lives, avoidance isn't going to reduce debt; it only delays engagement.

I need you to understand one very important point here: **debt is information. It is not a verdict.**

Let's repeat that together...

DEBT IS INFORMATION, NOT A VERDICT.

When you can accept that statement, then *a lot* of things about your financial life are going to change.

Debt is simply *information* about your financial past.

There are many things in your life (and your past) you didn't expect to happen, but they did.

You may have been confronted by:

- Unexpected expenses (we've detailed plenty of examples so far)
- Periods of instability
- Necessary borrowing during difficult seasons
- Decisions that made sense… *at the time*

I'll be the first to admit that some debt is the byproduct of mistakes. There's no doubt about it. You can't change that now. All you can do is move forward and deal with it.

Some debt is the result of circumstances. It could have been a medical crisis, being the victim of fraud, a robbery, or a scam, or even a repair bill that simply couldn't wait.

Most of our debt, though, is due to a combination of these two things. Regardless of *why* it's now data. Nothing more.

You can work with data.

WHY DEBT CAN FEEL OVERWHELMING

Debt creates a particular kind of psychological pressure[47]. Even though you are likely to have a number of regular financial obligations, those are finite. You pay them, it's done until the next month, quarter, or year.

Debt stretches out over time.

It represents past decisions that also affect your future. This ability for debt to span past, present, and future dimensions makes it feel permanent.

That's when some start to think, *"I'll never get out from under this debt."* Remember Michael? He felt the weight of debt when he couldn't keep

47 Debt and Mental Health (Mental Health Foundation). https://www.mentalhealth.org.uk/explore-mental-health/a-z-topics/debt-and-mental-health#:~:text=If%20you're%20depressed%2C%20you,debt%20can%20affect%20your%20sleep.

up with the bills. He took it personally, viewed it as a personal flaw and failure, and hid the truth from those he loved.

Interests accumulate more quickly as the balance grows higher. Any progress they make could be ripped away by another tight month or two when they can only pay down the minimum required payments.

When you feel trapped in that slow movement, it's easy to become discouraged. When that happens, they'll be more likely to avoid dealing with it in the future. This is why debt feels overwhelming.

And when it feels overwhelming, people may turn to a straightforward 'mathematical' approach to solving it (or trying to).

There are two main ways people tend to attempt to deal with or solve debt: mathematical strategies and human strategies.

If we just take a mathematical approach, the "best" way to eliminate debt is to prioritize your debts based on tackling your highest interest rates first. This (in theory and perfect execution) means the debt will accumulate slower, giving them time to bring it down.

Doing this minimizes the total interest paid over time. Interest is basically the cost of the debt. How much you pay for the privilege of borrowing.

The problem is that human behavior rarely follows mathematical logic. When you're overwhelmed or discouraged, motivation is fragile. Ergo, your fast brain won't care about mathematics. It wants immediate relief.

The human strategy offers an alternative, and that focuses on eliminating smaller balances first.

That gives you something to celebrate sooner as you see the small balance dwindling and then eventually reaching zero.

It builds confidence and confidence keeps people engaged.

The right strategy isn't always the one that looks best on paper. Sometimes it's the one that understands you and how you respond to various stimuli, successes, and setbacks.

PROGRESS THAT FEELS REAL

One of the great struggles that we tend to face when trying to tackle a fair amount of debt is that progress can *feel* slow.

If you're starting this journey deep in debt, you could realistically be looking at months of payments that seem to barely make a dent.

However, it's important to focus on what will work best ***for you***.

I have found that the human strategy of focusing on the smallest balance truly does work. You may have five debt accounts totaling $20,000, for example.

Your smallest balance could be $1,256. If you simply pay the minimum required payment on the other four debts, but then put whatever you have left toward the smallest balance, you'll watch that balance drop.

After your first month, it may be $1,135. Then after the second month it's $1,044. Then after the third month it's $952.

Just look at those numbers for a moment:

- $1,256
- $1,135
- $1,044
- $952

The final number in our example was three digits instead of four. It *looks* like progress.

When you measure progress of any kind, you'll begin to notice a change in stress levels when scanning your balances and accounts. Your confidence levels start to climb and believe you're actually going to be able to do this. You develop a clearer understanding of your financial priorities.

When your focus is on **real-world progress**, you can avoid the **all-or-nothing trap**.

That's when people approach their debt with an all-or-nothing mindset. They believe they need to tackle this whole thing quickly… or not at all.

By going with the all-or-nothing mindset, you'll need extreme focus. You would need to have aggressive payments and likely severe restrictions. That *might* work well temporarily, but for some, it's very difficult to maintain.

Sustainable **debt reduction** occurs within the middle ground. That means developing a system that is balanced with a life that remains livable.

In other words, you don't need to sacrifice everything you enjoy or care about to get financial balance into your life. So don't fall for the all-or-nothing trap.

That's where things shifted for Michael. He began working with a financial system that made sense for him, that helped him not just financially, but emotionally.

Within a couple of years, he and his wife managed to pay all their debts. All by making this subtle shift in strategy.

THE EMOTIONAL COST OF DEBT

You've already recognized that debt costs more than money. It affects more than just bank accounts.

It affects daily life.

When people carry debt, they often report:

- Increased stress levels
- Difficulty relaxing, even on vacation or days off from work
- Hesitation about future plans
- A persistent sense of unfinished business

Debt represents obligations that stretch well beyond today. That is going to have some emotional cost attached to it, but the cost will start to diminish when you develop a workable, manageable plan to tackle that debt.

It's going to diminish even before you start to make significant progress working the debt down.

PERSONAL ACTION STEP 15: DEBT STRAIN

If you're dealing with multiple debts –it doesn't matter if they are credit card related, mortgage, personal loans, etc.— it's a good idea to step back and evaluate them through three simple questions.

1. **Which debt causes the most stress when I think about it?**
   Emotional relief matters. Reducing the most stressful obligation can create mental breathing room. And you know how important *breathing room* can be.

2. **Which debt offers the most flexibility?**
   Some obligations allow extra payments without penalties. Some may also allow you to lower your minimum payments for now. When you have flexibility, this offers you more options and that makes these obligations easier to target.

3. **Which progress would feel most motivating?**
   When you *feel* like you're getting somewhere, as though you're actually gaining ground in the battle to pay down your debts, it's going to be a powerful incentive to keep pressing on.

When you take your current debt obligations and work on them through these three questions, it should provide an outline of a decent starting point.

Now, everyone is different and what works for one person may not be the best option for someone else. That's why you need to work on these questions honestly.

When you do, you should be able to see the right starting point.

Is the debt that's causing you the most stress what you should tackle first? If it's a mortgage, for example, and it's going to take you 20 years to pay down based on your current income, what happens to the rest of your debt?

Of course, if you're already behind and that's why it's causing you stress, then definitely that's something to put toward the top of your list.

Do you have some smaller debts, like a credit card or two, with balances of only a few hundred or a couple thousand dollars? Are you the type of person who gets pumped up from small victories?

Then that might be *your* optimal starting point.

Whatever you do, just make sure it aligns with *your* values, *your* expectations, and *your* financial situation.

Aarav The Serenity Genie™ will celebrate the small victories with you and guide you along this path to reducing and eventually removing your debt. It's a great supportive companion that offers daily encouragement, insight, and gentle nudges.

DEBT REPAYMENT IS NOT A RACE

It's important to financial peace. Absolutely.

But you're not winning this race tonight.

It's better to think of debt repayment as a long walk. There will be times when progress comes faster and times when it seems to crawl along. That's fine.

Stay the course.

Life is going to throw unexpected curves and obstacles in your way. Anticipate that. Expect them.

And keep going.

You're probably not going to feel like a new person when the debt is finally gone (or at least well manageable). You probably won't feel any kind of massive transformation.

But freedom will slip in through the front door of your life and make itself known.

A payment suddenly disappears from your monthly list. The balance on a bloated debt finally seems manageable. Financial decisions begin to feel lighter.

You notice the absence of financial and emotional weight, and that may be one of the best benefits of all.

Debt deserves your attention. If you're carrying debt and don't have financial peace, this **must** be addressed and handled.

Whatever debt you currently carry, it's only a chapter of your financial story; it's not the entire book.

Work on it.

I highly recommend the path of starting with your smallest balance first, but do what will be best for you. And stick with it.

If it doesn't work, if that plan places too much stress and pressure on you, **adjust**. Try another approach.

When you find the one that works for you, stick with it until the end and you will notice a positive and emotionally healthy change in your life.

CHAPTER 15

Investing When You're Starting Late... Or Small

It's not too late — and small still counts.

— — —

Jake and Martha were stretched financially. It caused a lot of strain on their relationship, and by the time they were in their mid-50s, their two children off to college, they worried about the future, especially about their retirement.

Martha would listen to podcasts and read books and glean information from a wide range of sources, all about finances, and though they learned a lot, it never seemed to make a real difference in real life.

They were still staring down the barrel of difficult financial times in their late 60s, 70s, and (hopefully) beyond.

They managed to provide for their family, raised their kids, sent them off to college, and bought a house later in life.

But they began worrying more about the future.

The economy was strong. Things hadn't looked better in years. The stock market was soaring.

Yet something didn't seem right to them. John began to learn about finances and he and Martha had long conversations about their situation and their future. But they never really put that knowledge to work for them. Even though they understood that investing was the key to unlocking the future they wanted, they both struggled to get past the feeling it was 'too late.'

At their age, they thought, "What difference would it make if they started now?"

Throughout their 30s and 40s, and even to this point in their life, *investing* was always something they assumed they'd "get around to." But they hadn't.

Now, any time they would think about investing, they thought of it as more about **missed opportunities** than a chance to grow wealth.

Jake and Martha are no different than millions of people in their 40s, 50s, and 60s who feel a sense of embarrassment about investing simply because they never 'got around to it' when it 'mattered.'

Much of the advice surrounding investing says to "**start early.**"

That same advice talks about how compounding interest rewards those who start early the most. They hear about people who invested $1,000 a month throughout their 20s while starting their career and ended up with millions of dollars for their retirement.

Most people *don't* start investing at that age. Many don't even really get to invest in their 30s, either. Sure, they might partake in an investment program their employer has in place (like a 401(k) in the United States), but there's some volatility in that, and people often worry about the stock market, recessions, and unexpected circumstances that could negatively impact the final number when they retire.

While the advice about starting early is sound and even spot on, what does it tend to do for people like Jake and Martha who *didn't* get started early?

It's not like we have a reset button or can rewind our life and start over. We only have one life, so what happens if you missed the boat?

Maybe you begin to think:

- *I should have started years ago* (thus compounding guilt in your financial life).
- *What difference would a small amount even make?* (So, you don't bother starting.)
- *Everyone else is already so far ahead.* (That assumes competition, even though there is no competition with investors.)
- Then what happens? You postpone starting. Maybe you tell yourself several excuses, like:
- "I'll get started when I have more money," or,
- "I'll do this when I feel more stable financially," or,
- "I'll think about this when I'm more confident."

There's a reason this feels familiar—and why it keeps repeating (whether it *already* happened or hasn't yet). Lots of people hit an "analysis paralysis" because they worry about making mistakes. "Cognitive biases can act as barriers that prevent people from getting started with investing, and keep them on the sidelines for too long[48]."

When you let months and even years slip by, *thinking* and *knowing* you should invest, but never get started, it's not about laziness.

It's about discouragement.

48 Marc Guberti. The Real Reason Many People Miss Out on Years of Investment Growth (Money). Mar. 8, 2026. https://money.com/why-smart-people-wait-too-long-to-invest/#:~:text=But%20even%20people%20with%20a,may%20help%20you%20overcome%20them.

THE PROBLEM WITH THE "START EARLY" NARRATIVE

One of the most common pieces of financial advice is simple: start investing as early as possible.

There's nothing wrong with that advice.

Compound growth rewards time more than almost anything else and the earlier money enters the system, the more opportunity it has to grow.

But this advice has an unintended side effect. For the hundreds of millions of people around the world who *didn't* start early, it can create this notion (or feeling) that the opportunity has already slipped past them.

Instead of being encouraged, they hear a verdict. Then it's easy to think, "If I missed the ideal moment, then what's the point?"

That entire way of thinking relates to believing there's a **perfect beginning** for investing.

It's easy to assume that investing begins with a significant step, a perfect step at the optimal time. This ideal beginning might include:

- A large initial contribution
- A carefully researched portfolio
- A moment when everything feels financially settled

What most of us don't see, however, is the reality of many investment journeys.

It's kind of like watching a professional athlete, being in awe of his or her physical abilities, stamina, discipline, and focus.

What we don't see are the years and years of practice, dedication, and failure just to get to that point. We assume we would *never* have been able to do anything *close* to what they do. And we make that assumption not because we understand our own abilities, but because we see the result, not the years of tireless practice and failure and striving leading up to it.

Regarding investing, we hear stories about amassed wealth through investing, early retirement success stories because of a person's foresight, and tales of how someone followed their investments, learned the industry, and mastered their money with hours of daily devotion to it.

In reality, most investment journeys begin far more modestly. They start with small number, with people who have little to no understanding about any of it, and with a host of uncertainty.

The difference between people who build wealth through investments and those who don't has nothing to do with the size of that first step or their knowledge or their level of certainty.

It has to do with a willingness to take that first step.

SMALL BEGINNINGS MATTER

One of the toughest things to wrap your head around is that small contributions may *feel* insignificant, but they matter. Compared to those large numbers you might hear about in the financial news outlets, small beginnings serve a very valuable purpose.

They shift your identity.

If it's only $25 a month to start, that's great! That small bit makes you an **investor**! What if it's only $10? That's a great beginning!

When you start on this path to investing, even with very little to start with, you move from thinking, "Investing is something I'll do *someday*" to thinking, "I'm someone who invests."

Behavior has a tendency to follow identity[49]. If you think of yourself as someone who 'missed the boat,' you'll live like someone who 'missed the boat.'

If you think of yourself as someone who 'saves,' then you'll save.

If you think of yourself as an 'investor,' then you'll invest.

One of the most common harmful assumptions that surround investing is the idea that success depends on how much money you contribute.

Sure, if you're able to pour more money into *sound, solid* investments, that's going to pay more dividends over time. However, it's important to understand that **consistency matters more**.

Regular contributions –no matter how modest —create ***momentum***. That allows the compounding aspect of investments to get rolling. It also starts forming habits that become easier over time.

It's the habits that will create lasting change. That's what Jake and Martha discovered when they finally started in this manner, with small numbers at first.

It didn't produce major returns for years, but by the time they reached retirement age, they had accumulated enough for the plans they wanted to pursue.

I want you to think of investing as a rhythm rather than as some singular decision to make once (or twice here and there).

Small, repeated actions accumulate quietly. What may *feel* small today can become significant and meaningful later simply because it continued.

49 Alfrey, Condie, and Rebar. The Influence of Identity Within-Person and Between Behaviours: A 12-Week Repeated Measures Study (National Library of Medicine). May 3, 2025. https://pmc.ncbi.nlm.nih.gov/articles/PMC12109062/

THE PSYCHOLOGICAL BARRIER OF COMPARISON

There are going to be plenty of reasons why you may struggle to get started investing. Maybe you did a little in the past and lost, or didn't gain much.

Perhaps the small amount you invested has been slowly increasing, but it's not anything you're going to bank on in your later years.

But if you're like most of the rest of us, you've never *really* got going with investing, and that could very well be because of **comparison**.

When we hear about large portfolios, hundreds of thousands or even millions of dollars in value, it's natural to compare ourselves to that. We tend to measure our success against those examples. When we look at where those successful people are and see where we are (or aren't, more likely), the gap is high.

That leads to discouragement[50].

Yet comparison rarely considers context. And there's a whole lot of context that needs to be considered here.

- Some people started investing earlier.
- Some had higher starting incomes.
- Some didn't have financial responsibilities like you had.
- Some received financial support that others never saw (like from an inheritance or parents, etc.).

Comparing your starting point to someone else's mid or even finish line is unfair to you. That's like comparing your abilities as a hobbyist athlete to a professional in their prime.

50 The Psychology of Comparison: Why We Do It and How to Stop Now and in the Future (Mindful Health Solutions). Nov. 3, 2023. https://mindfulhealth-solutions.com/the-psychology-of-comparison-why-we-do-it-and-how-to-stop/#:~:text=A%20frequent%20side%2Deffect%20of,your%20own%20capabilities%20and%20worth.

The only meaningful comparison you should be making is between your present and your past. And, mostly, just between where you were yesterday compared to today.

Progress begins where you are… now.

KEEPING INVESTING SIMPLE

Another key reason why so many of us fail to get started with investing is complexity.

Financial terminology alone can be intimidating. Terms like:

- Asset allocation
- Diversification
- Capital gain
- Bull market
- Risk tolerance
- Bear market
- And so on…

When confronted with so many choices about the types of accounts and all that terminology, it's easy to respond by stepping back and avoiding the endeavor altogether.

What you need to remember is that perfect understanding rarely ever comes before experience.

More important to keep in mind is that many successful investors follow remarkably simple strategies. They prioritize diversification (having your investments in multiple accounts, companies, or other funds), consistency (avoiding pushing and pulling money in and out constantly, and patience.

Simplicity will tend to outperform sophistication over long periods of time.

These days, we have automated tools that can simplify investing. You can set up automatic contributions, so it doesn't depend on your mood, anxiety, or doubt. The system would continue operating on autopilot.

Automation removes the emotional friction that tends to accompany manual decisions. Instead of stressing over whether you should invest each month, the decision is made once and then repeated.

Before you know it, you've shifted from investing occasionally with worry and doubt to an ongoing process that will tend to produce positive growth over time.

MANAGE EXPECTATIONS

Keep your expectations realistic.

There's so much fiction surrounding the world of investment and finance, movies and television programs and novels, and so forth that make it seems as though *everyone* is doing *great* and making tons of money with their investments.

That's not how the real world works. Markets rise and fall. Returns fluctuate. Progress rarely follows a straight-line path.

People who expect constant upward movement often become discouraged during the inevitable downturns.

However, when you understand volatility is simply a part of the nature of investing, you'll feel steadier.

Patience isn't just a virtue in investing; it's a requirement. Over long periods of time, consistency tends to matter more than timing, and therein lies lasting peace and serenity.

PERSONAL ACTION STEP 16: SMALL NUMBERS, BIG GAINS

If investing feels intimidating, I want you to start with one simple question:

> ***What is the smallest amount I could invest regularly <u>without</u> disrupting my stability (or cutting into my breathing room)?***

For some, that number may be $10 a month. For others, it might be $25. For others, it may be $100.

The actual number isn't the important factor here: it's the **pattern** that will form when you finally start.

Beginning small is *not* a sign of weakness.

It's a sign of momentum.

Aarav The Serenity Genie™ will listen to you, where you are now, and help you build a track toward your future goals.

THE QUIET POWER OF TIME

Time is the most powerful ally with investing[51]. That's not because it produces dramatic changes overnight (investments), but because it allows **small** actions to accumulate.

A single contribution rarely feels significant. But just think about any small thing by itself, whether it's a few flakes of snow compressed in your hand that, when rolled through more heavy snow becomes bigger and bigger until it could crush through a fortress.

51 Ryan Ermey. Every young person should see this chart and understand their 'greatest money-making asset' (CNBC Make It). Aug. 12, 2022. https://www.cnbc.com/2022/08/12/chart-why-an-investors-greatest-asset-is-time.html#:~:text=If%20the%20investor%20who%20started,career%20with%20our%20weekly%20newsletter

Or an army of one isn't much of a threat, but when you have a million other soldiers aligned with that one, they become a force to be reckoned with.

Whatever small contributions you start with *will* likely grow, if you give it time, diversify, and are patient.

The key is to **participate**. You can't attain financial growth through investments if you don't invest.

Yes, it's natural to wish you had started earlier. But you didn't. And that's okay.

Whether you're 25 or 30, 40, 50, 60, or even 70 or 80, **it's not too late**!

Regret about the past never improves your future. The only moment that matters for getting started is right now.

You can't recover the years before today. But you can make sure today is not another missed opportunity.

Get the habit started as soon as you have breathing room and some extra money each month. Once it does, the question about what it's "too late" becomes moot.

What matters then is that you started!

WHERE WE GO NEXT

Investing introduces the possibility of long-term growth. Unfortunately for many people, income has become less predictable.

Next, we're going to look at the 'gig' economy and how it affects financial stability and how to navigate income volatility without sacrificing mental health or long-term progress.

For now, I want you to remember that:

- You don't need a perfect starting point.
- You don't need a large amount of money.
- You simply need to begin.

Can you do that? I know you can, and that's awesome.

Remember: small beginnings, repeated over time, are how **lasting** *financial progress* is made.

Like a building, you take the first brick or beam and set it in place, then another and another and another until you have a strong, formidable building.

So, get building!

CHAPTER 16

Burning Through the Gig Economy

More income doesn't help if it burns you out.

— — —

THE GLOBAL ECONOMY HAS CHANGED. HOW PEOPLE EARN MONEY throughout nearly every corner of the world has shifted. Sometimes dramatically so.

For those who had (and still have) the traditional pattern of work (whether farming or working set, fixed hours for a predictable amount of money per hour, month, or year), it might be difficult to understand the changing landscape of earnings and income.

Many people have discovered a more fluid and liberalized way of earning money and it's commonly referred to today as the **gig economy**.

"The gig economy, also known as the sharing or access economy, features temporary, freelance, and part-time positions often filled by independent contractors (Investopedia)[52]."

In other words, freelancing, consulting, contract work, side projects, and short-term jobs have become increasingly common parts of the financial landscape.

While these types of work opportunities offer flexibility and independence, there's a lack of security associated with them. In some countries where employers provide health and even investment benefits to full-time workers, that's typically not a benefit gig workers enjoy.

Companies can save a lot of money by hiring freelancers for *only* the work they need and save on hiring costs and other benefits.

Many people enjoy the perceived freedom they get from working in a gig economy. It allows them to work *when* they want or need, to work from home if they want, and control more aspects of their daily life.

But it can feel exhausting.

Income becomes less predictable. The boundaries between personal and professional life gets blurred. Work doesn't just follow you home; it often is done at home. And there's always another opportunity, another project, another adjustment that needs to be made, and of course there's always another opportunity to earn more to cover your next expense or bill or vacation.

Plus, there's also always another chance to slip up, slack off, and find yourself falling behind on work and income.

52 Margaret James. Understanding the Gig Economy: Flexible Jobs Explained (Investopedia). Aug. 20, 2025 (fact checked by Katrina Munichello). https://www.investopedia.com/terms/g/gig-economy.asp

THE PROMISE AND THE REALITY

In 2026, it's estimated that there are 1.57 ***billion*** people engaged in freelance work globally. That is nearly *half* of the global workforce[53].

The gig economy is often hailed for the possibilities it opens up to the average worker.

Some of those benefits include:

- You can work when you want,
- You can choose the projects you'll enjoy working on,
- You can build multiple streams of income.

The possibilities are real for many people, but that kind of flexibility comes with a tradeoff.

Income can (and often does) fluctuate dramatically from one month to the next. Any benefits you may have had from a fixed employer – whether it had to do with health or retirement or sick time or vacation days— is a thing of the past (you become responsible for all of that). If you're sick and can't work and your previous job still paid you for X number of days during the year when you were ill, with the gig economy, 'You don't work, you don't get paid.'

Managing your work schedule, discipling yourself to put the time in each day, receiving payments, taxes, and more all shift solely onto your lap.

This combination of freedom and responsibility can create a unique kind of financial tension.

You are in control (yeah!), but you are also *always* responsible… for everything (yuk!).

53 Richard Jaimes. Freelancing Statistics 2026 (Quantrum Foresight). Nov. 7, 2025. https://www.quantumrun.com/consulting/freelancing-statistics/

WHEN HUSTLE BECOMES HABIT

I don't want you to assume that this gig economy is the optimal solution to all your financial challenges. Yes, there is the possibility to earn more than you're bringing in now (or did) with a typical 40 or 30 or 50-hour workweek.

However, the results aren't always positive.

If you're not earning enough with freelance or consulting work, for example, you may be told to:

- Take another job.
- Pick up more clients.
- Work longer hours.

For short periods of time, this approach can be effective. Additional work, more bids on projects, more time put into the effort to secure jobs can have a positive and immediate impact on your income. That can certainly relieve financial pressure.

However, when your hustle becomes a *permanent* strategy, something important begins to erode.

Your energy.

And, as we've seen already, when energy levels drop, your body gives your brain certain signals, and your brain will shift into a pattern of seeking fast relief from the stress and strain of the moment.

We're not built for continuous acceleration. Without proper time to rest and recover, productivity will naturally start to decline. Creativity fades. And burnout eventually worms its way into the corners of your life.

It's ironic; the pursuit of financial stability by going this path has the potential to undermine personal stability.

THE DIFFERENCE BETWEEN SURVIVAL WORK AND STRATEGIC WORK

It's important that we not get confused and assume all work is the same (or that it serves the same purpose).

When you're under financial pressure, you may look for odd local jobs that may be available to help. Part-time and temporary assignments are normal for people feeling financial pain and who seek short-term relief.

The problem with this plan (or approach) is that it's not feasible to sustain long-term.

You may deal with irregular hours, emotional labor, or physical strain (depending on the type of 'gig work' you take on). Relying heavily on **survival** work often leads to exhaustion, and too often it doesn't provide any real lasting financial security.

That's why we need to think about ***strategic*** work instead.

The ultimate goal when it comes to any type of income stream is *predictability.* When you can enjoy a predictable income on a regular basis, then you have the foundation for peace.

In order to accomplish this, you may have to develop or enhance your current skillset. You may need to focus on building strong relationships with clients (or new clients you haven't even met yet). Or find different avenues that will offer more steady and predictable income.

There are benefits to gig work. There are also challenges that go along with it. The goal for us should be finding the right balance that allows survival today without sacrificing sustainability tomorrow.

THE PROBLEM WITH ALWAYS BEING "ON"

When you turn to the gig economy for your main income, you'll eventually reach a point when it seems as though you are always ***on***.

The line between your working hours and personal time doesn't just become blurred, it can completely evaporate, leaving you feeling stressed and anxious all the time, since you'll be 'on the clock' almost all the time.

The doesn't mean you'll be working every waking moment, every day of the week, though. It means you may be talking to clients, fielding questions, bidding, contacting prospects, and more all the time.

There won't be any 'off' time if you're not careful.

Some examples of this constant 'always on' work may include:

- A message arriving late in the evening, and it's one you don't feel you can ignore.
- A potential client reaches out on the weekend with important questions, and you know if you wait until Monday to answer them, the job might very well go to someone else, someone more responsive.
- A new opportunity promises a little extra income, even though it'll mean having to work during your normal 'family' or 'down' time.

Even though each of these examples might seem small on the surface, over time, the cumulative effect will grow more significant. Your brain will start operating on a constant state of availability.

Rest becomes conditional. Relaxation feels temporary. Even the times when you get some quiet, or go on vacation, will have a tendril of stress running in the background. You might believe, subconsciously, that you should be more productive.

This is going to drain both your energy and attention.

When you have an irregular income to deal with, what do you think (or know) it's going to do to your financial approach?

It's going to complicate them.

When earnings fluctuate, it's going to become more difficult to predict how much revenue you'll bring in next month, and some months might have more than you expected (which is always nice) and others will be far less than you need.

This volatility creates two opposing reactions. One the one hand, when months are strong, you might feel tempted to spend more freely, especially under the constant stress and strain of always being 'on.'

On other months, anxiety over your bills will increase. Spending tightens and plans might have to be postponed.

Your financial life becomes unpredictable, even *if* your total income for the year is relatively stable or even increasing.

What we've seen over and over is that when people under stress and strain have more disposable income (even if it's not really disposable, but more coming in one month), the chance of spending it increases, leaving you short the next.

We don't want to ignore the gig economy, though. It's valuable. The goal is to manage the balance more effectively.

THE TWO-GIG PRINCIPLE

An effective framework to manage gig-based income is the **two-gig principle**.

Instead of relying on unpredictable work, focus on seeking out two complementary income streams:

- A stabilizing source, and
- A flexible source.

The stabilizing source of income might be:

- A part-time job with consistent pay
- A long-term client
- A recurring service you provide regularly

This type of income will offer a baseline of predictable income.

The flexible source of income might be:

- Freelance projects
- Occasional consulting
- Creative or entrepreneurial ventures

This type of income would add opportunity without carrying the entire burden of financial security in your life. When you have two streams like this, it will create structure that balances stability with flexibility.

This would also help you protect your energy, which can be a financial resource of its own.

That's right. Even though our first thought about financial resources is money, there's also energy.

When you don't have sufficient energy in your daily life, your productivity levels will likely diminish, your ability to make sound decisions might falter, and creativity will often decline.

When you burn out while working in the gig economy, it won't just affect your physical or emotional or mental well-being; it can affect your financial outcomes.

Protecting your energy, then, means you need to create boundaries around your work and personal life. Rest is not a waste of time; it's about recovery so you can go forth with clarity and proper levels of energy.

Just like money needs to circulate wisely (investing), energy needs to be maintained carefully.

PLANNING FOR VOLATILITY

If you can't remove unpredictability from your financial life, then you can forge into it some anticipation strategies. These may include:

- Building small buffers during the stronger months
- Maintaining a simplified financial system that can adapt relatively quickly and easily
- Prioritizing essential expenses when income varies

You're not going to eliminate volatility completely, but you can reduce the emotional impact they might have on you and your family.

When you rely on the gig economy, no two months will be or look the same financially. That's okay, so long as you find a way to manage them in a way that works best for you.

One major challenge people deal with in the gig economy is that its tendency is for short-term thinking.

Projects come and go quickly. You have to continually 'keep the funnel' full, meaning you need to keep seeking out the next projects. Payments arrive irregularly and sometimes you have to chase down clients to get paid.

Sometimes it would be a good idea to step back and evaluate the larger picture, especially considering your financial situation, past tendencies, and future goals. Our goal should always be serenity, even in the midst of a hostile world.

PERSONAL ACTION STEP 17: GIG REFLECTIONS

Not everyone will be participating in the gig economy, but with almost half the global workforce diving in, this section is still relevant to most readers.

If you have started or tried to participate in the gig economy, and if you've been pleased with the process and progress so far, I want you to step back every month or so and ask these three questions:

1. Which work produces the most reliable income?
2. Which work produces the most exhaustion?
3. Which opportunities align with the life I want to build?

Answering these questions honestly will provide some insight into the types of projects you enjoy, which ones offer better stability and growth, and which ones have been draining you emotionally, mentally, physically, and/or financially.

Keep these questions with you.

Serenity Aligned™ (see back of book) will allow you to set a reminder to evaluate your situation each month or two.

When you come up with your answers, you can take action that will bring you closer to your own long-term work and income-related goals.

MOVING FORWARD WITH INTENTION

You may have heard that working in freelance or as a consultant offers endless growth, freedom to decide when and where and with whom you work, and that always sounds amazing.

In reality, it can be difficult, especially in the beginning. So don't think success can be measured by steady growth or a specific number earned for a month.

Instead, look at the big picture. Success might mean having an income that feels steady enough to plan around, work that allows you enough time to rest and refresh, and financial systems that support long-term stability.

Success is not about working more, but working in a way you can sustain over time.

The gig economy is here to stay. If you dive into these waters, just remember to maintain balance, structure, and realistic expectations.

Flexibility should ***support*** your life, not consume it.

Part Four

A Calmer Financial Future

CHAPTER 17

Measuring Progress Without Obsession

Progress is quieter than you think.

— — —

For Thomas, he didn't tend to struggle with his finances, not in the way many people do.

He became almost obsessive about tracking his finances. For him, it felt empowering.

The stress that had overwhelmed him because no matter what he earned, no matter the raises and promotions, it never seemed like enough. Tracking his spending helped bring some clarity.

When you're finally able to get to a position of stability, you might:

- Start tracking spending,
- Check your accounts regularly,
- Review your plans and goals.

That is certainly what Thomas started doing. However, a small shift also began to take shape in his world. Thomas began to check his balances several times a day. Small fluctuations started to trigger worry. Progress started to feel fragile and he was thinking every bit of success he had achieved could be stripped away by one unexpected expense.

What had appeared to be support was still anxiety, even though it was dressed in finer clothes.

While his efforts started out as promising financial peace, and it did for a time, it morphed into another form of stress.

This is the risk that ***over***-monitoring poses.

Thomas stumbled into that tragedy because constantly watching money, accounts, and counting every single penny can make one *feel* as though they're in control. Even when they're not.

THE ILLUSION OF CONTROL

Keeping track of your financial data offers a potentially powerful psychological effect. Monitoring your finances promotes emotional stability, builds confidence, and encourages more sound decisions[54].

Numbers feel objective. What you see is what you get. Isn't it nice when you look at your cashflow or bank account and *know* precisely what you have in there? Especially when there's enough to cover your current bills and still leaves you with some breathing room.

54 School of Accountancy, Henan Institute of Economics and Trade, Zhengzhou, Henan, China. Impact of financial literacy, mental budgeting and self control on financial wellbeing: Mediating impact of investment decision making (National Library of Medicine). Nov. 14, 2018. https://pmc.ncbi.nlm.nih.gov/articles/PMC10645357/#:~:text=Moreover%2C%20individuals%20who%20practice%20mental,wellness%20and%20enhance%20financial%20results.

Numbers give us the impression that if we watch them close enough, we can prevent unpleasant surprises.

At this point in our time together, I trust that you've already seen some progress. No matter how large or small your steps, whether it's just one small step or several bigger ones you've made, I'm sure you've begun to experience the positive effects that tracking *something* offers.

You've felt a little control slip back into your life, right?

But it's essential that you remember that watching numbers –by itself— isn't going to change any outcome. Inflation can hit suddenly. Markets will fluctuate. Bills arrive and sometimes they're bigger than you expected or anticipated, throwing your carefully manicured plans into a little turmoil.

Life is messy. It introduces uncertainty.

No matter how diligent or religious you are about tracking your numbers, none of that changes.

You *can* shift from monitoring in a healthy manner to something more constant, something obsessive. You may not even recognize monitoring as a problem for a long time because it looks like vigilance.

And vigilance, for many of us, equals control. But when you are feeling the need to **constantly** track and monitor everything all the time, you're no longer in control.

In that situation, you've slipped into volatility all over again. This time, though, the volatility is about trying to hold firm control in a system that was built to handle small changes, designed to help you navigate and anticipate minor setbacks, but you fall into a state of constant worry and panic… for all the wrong reasons.

The result is a cycle of hyperattention that drains energy without improving decisions.

Hey, there's no doubt that financial awareness is valuable. It absolutely is. When you awaken awareness about your finances, then you're able to see patterns, catch problems early, and make informed decisions that align with your values, purpose, and goals.

But I want you to remember that there is a significant difference between awareness and **surveillance**.

- Awareness involves periodic review.
- Surveillance involves **constant** observation.
- Awareness creates clarity.
- Surveillance creates tension.

You can get a very real sense that your relationship with money has changed when you start making progress, regardless of the size of that progress. And you will be more aware of the details associated with your money and bills and outflow. When you shift to surveillance, you'll begin to feel strained again.

This time, though, it's not caused by ignorance but by overexposure.

Think of it like a parent and child.

As a child grows up, the parent(s) teach him or her. They offer guidance and firm boundaries the younger they are. As the child moves into their pre-teen and teenage years, though, a shift begins to take shape.

The young individual starts to gain more independence, but also more responsibility. A doting parent will still want to guide and teach and protect their child, but also allow them room to discover things on their own.

There is increased risk with each passing year, but also increased growth and maturity (hopefully).

A parent is going to monitor their child. They'll follow up with their child's friends' parents to make sure they are where they said they'd be, are doing what they said they'd be doing, and so on.

Over time, a parent can choose to *trust* their child and let go of the *constant* monitoring or become overbearing.

An overbearing parent is eventually going to find that his or her child will push back, become combative, 'moody,' seemingly distant, and fighting over small things more and more.

While money isn't going to care if you're over-monitoring like a child would as they get older, *you* are going to find yourself more stressed, more anxious, and falling into similar traps you found yourself in some time ago.

Too much attention to *anything* in life will tend to magnify each fluctuation, each ripple in the water, every single hiccup in your finances.

Like a parent becoming overbearing to their children, they'll begin to notice each white lie, small attitude growing bigger, and even the silence between them growing more pronounced.

And none of this is because you're a controlling person. It's because your brain is wired for feedback loops.

WHY THE BRAIN SEEKS CONSTANT UPDATES

This urge to check numbers frequently has a neurological basis. The brain is specifically wired for feedback loops. It acts as a self-regulating system that constantly gathers information, processes that information, and updates internal models and determines proper actions[55].

You can see this in your own body every day. When you're hot, you sweat (your body's natural way of trying to cool its core temperature).

55 Dan Docherty. The Science of Feedback: How to Deliver It in a Way That Sticks (Braintrust). Jan. 29, 2025: https://www.quantumrun.com/consulting/freelancing-statistics/

When you're cold, you shiver (your body's natural way of trying to increase blood flow, which brings up core temperatures).

It's the same with your mental well-being; your brain *wants* to be calm. It *wants* things to go well for you.

If you know anything about modern technology and social media (Facebook, Tik Tok, X, etc.), and you participate in these ecosystems, then you're aware of the 'likes' and 'shares' and heart icons that people tap on topics or posts or pictures they like.

For the one posting on social media, they may check back frequently to see how many people 'liked' it. Younger generations are currently dealing with an obsessive tendency to check their social accounts for that **feedback loop**.

If friends aren't 'liking' or following or viewing their content, it can create anxiety and stress and may make that person think no one cares about them.

When you're constantly checking numbers (which is much easier today because of banking apps and investment dashboards you might have on your smartphone), you might well be tempted to check them daily.

- Then a couple of times a day –morning and night.
- Then a few times throughout the day.
- Then every other hour.
- Then every hour.
- Before you know it, you're ***constantly*** obsessive over it, especially because it has become so simple and convenient to do so.

I knew a person who invested money in various stocks and bonds. We met up one day while on vacation as we just happened to be in the same city at the same approximate time.

Even though he was with family, on vacation, I witnessed him constantly looking at his phone, not for social media or news, but the stock market performance.

He wasn't buying or selling. He wasn't trading. There was nothing he could do to affect the performance of his investments.

Yet, he had slipped into an obsessive trap, and he was missing out on valuable time with his family.

When you're getting some new trinkets of information, new insights about your money, it can feel great. It provides a small sense of certainty, right?

Even if the information you get doesn't change or affect anything, it just... ***feels*** good.

You've gotten a small sense of reassurance. *'Everything's okay,'* it says. *'Everything's going well.'*

Don't you want to have that same positive reinforcement again?

Given enough time, this type of behavior can become a habit and not all habits are good ones.

Constant updates rarely improve long-term outcomes. They only amplify short-term emotional reactions.

"The human brain is naturally wired to seek rewards and avoid threats. This means that feedback, especially when it is critical, can trigger the brain's amygdala, the part of the brain responsible for the fight-or-flight response. When this happens, the prefrontal cortex, which governs rational thinking and problem-solving, is momentarily overridden, making it harder for individuals to process and apply feedback effectively (Braintrust)[56]."

56 Dan Docherty. The Science of Feedback: How to Deliver It in a Way That Sticks (Braintrust). Jan. 29, 2025: https://www.quantumrun.com/consulting/freelancing-statistics/

THE COST OF OVER-TRACKING

The moment your financial attention becomes *excessive*, it runs the risk of producing several unintended consequences.

- First of those is **stress**. By constantly tracking your money, any shift in the numbers can make progress seem fragile, even if the long-term trends are still moving in the right direction.
- Second, it reduces your perspective down to a narrow viewpoint. It becomes difficult to notice meaningful patterns over time because you're always so focused on the small, minor changes.
- Third, it drains mental energy. Your brain spends so much effort processing information that doesn't often require any action on your part.

If this goes on long enough, it can cause someone to be discouraged from continuing with their financial system because the emotional load just becomes too heavy to carry.

Not all financial metrics are the same, or equally useful. Some numbers will help guide your decision-making processes. Others may provide information without requiring action.

When you're monitoring too many metrics, there's a real risk of getting confused. The numeric 'noise' becomes too much.

The goal of financial measurement and monitoring isn't to gather *as much information as possible*. It's to **identify** the information that actually helps guide your behaviors.

By focusing on fewer metrics, you may find it easier to come to clear decisions.

PERSONAL ACTION STEP: CHOOSING THE RIGHT SIGNALS

Let's focus on just a few key signals to monitor in your personal financial journey right now.

- Cash-flow stability
- Reduce avoidance
- Faster recovery from setbacks

Ask yourself three simple questions associated with these three key signals:

- Are your monthly obligations consistently manageable? (Cash-flow stability)
- Are you more comfortable looking at your finances than you were before? (Reduced avoidance)
- When unexpected expenses occur, do you recover more quickly now? (Faster recovery from setbacks)

These signals might not produce dramatic results, but they do reflect ***real progress.*** Serenity Aligned™ (see back of book) has these questions and a few more that will help you move forward with better clarity while avoiding the trap of over-tracking.

Financial health is not just about accumulation. It's about resilience.

Traditional financial metrics, such as net worth, savings rates, and investment balances, are valuable insights, but they don't capture **emotional stability**.

You might have two people with identical financial numbers who experience their financial lives very differently. One may constantly be anxious while the other is calm and confident.

The difference is the relationship each person has with money.

So, remember, progress includes the emotional outcomes as well as the numerical data.

When you start on this journey, don't be focused on immediate leaps and bounds. Progress is going to be gradual.

Trying to force something to change too quickly can lead to stress and anxiety. Real progress unfolds slowly.

- Savings accumulate gradually.
- Debt balances decline incrementally.
- Investments grow unevenly, but they grow, over time.

If you get to the point where you're expecting rapid visible results, you'll likely become discouraged by normal fluctuations and the natural tendency for things to move more slowly than that.

It's easier to be patient when your expectations match reality.

CREATE HEALTHY REVIEW RHYTHMS

I don't want you *constantly* monitoring. Instead, create regular review rhythms.

These might include:

- A brief weekly check-in to review spending and upcoming bills.
- A monthly review of overall financial progress.
- A quarterly review of larger goals and adjustments.

These kinds of rhythms will allow you to stay informed without being overwhelmed.

Keep in mind that the purpose of financial awareness is not to think about money all the time, but to think about money *less*.

When your systems work properly, your financial life should become quieter. Decisions will be easier. Your attention will move away from every bill, every worry, and every doubt toward other, more important parts of life.

It's ironic, though, that the best financial systems are the ones that eventually require less attention.

PERSONAL ACTION STEP 18: MODERATION

I want you to try a small experiment *IF* you find yourself checking financial numbers frequently.

Choose **ONE** type of financial information –it might be your checking account balance, investments, regular bills, etc.— and *reduce* how often you look at it.

If you tend to check something daily, try once a week.

If you check weekly, then try only checking it monthly.

Then see what happens.

At first, you may have a strong desire to check that information. That's anxiety disguised as concern.

However, many people discover that their anxiety decreases when they take these steps.

Distance helps restore perspective. And Serenity Aligned™ (see back of book) helps you stay on track. Peacefully.

WHAT PROGRESS REALLY LOOKS LIKE

Financial progress isn't going to come barreling in like a train through the living room of your life. It's going to show up quietly.

It might look like:

- Worrying less about small purchases,
- Recovering from surprises more quickly,
- Feeling less urgency around every decision.

The numbers may improve, and that's great, but the most meaningful change to focus on at first is how money fits into your life.

When it occupies less mental space, that's a huge win. That is true success.

Thomas was given some friendly, sound advice from a colleague who noticed the change in her behavior at work. Her friend spotted her constant obsession over her accounts and money and suggested that she step back for a while.

It wasn't easy, but she tried. Each day she struggled, but eventually reached a point where she only needed to check-in once a week, and as a result, she felt peace returning to her life.

As we close in on the final chapters of this book, we're going to discover what money is ultimately meant to support: a satisfying and meaningful life.

For now, it's enough to remember:

Financial awareness is meant to create freedom, not fixation.

The goal is not to watch every number.

It's to build a life where you don't have to worry about that anymore.

CHAPTER 18

Money and Life Satisfaction

> *Money matters, but life satisfaction matters more.*

— — —

DO YOU KNOW WHAT MONEY IS *FOR*?

I don't mean things like paying the bills or creating some form of security in life. I don't even mean that money can allow some level of freedom.

That's what many people *assume* money is for, and while those things are true on some level, there's a deeper, more meaningful thing we tend to miss or overlook.

Yes, money is *used* for a number of things, especially where it relates to daily life. However, it's not just a resource.

Money is a **tool** that **shapes** daily life.

Think about that for a while. Before reading on, just meditate for one or two minutes on that statement:

Money is a *tool* that *shapes* daily life.

- The way we go about *earning* money.
- How we *spend* money.
- How we might *save* money.
- How some *invest* money.

These things all *influence* how we experience our lives, how we experience our days. This all impacts how much time we have throughout the days, where our focus tends to be, even when we're *not* working, trying to earn some money, how much stress we feel and endure, and how it can affect our personal relationships.

Do you know what the number one cause of relationships falling apart tends to be the world over?

Finances[57].

A husband and wife, married for twenty years, grow cold toward one another because the money is tight and the stress is always present and, as a result, they are bickering more and more. That bickering leads to arguments, which lead to fights, then silence and distance and then a falling away from which many don't recover.

Two best friends who once lived and thought like actual brothers slip into the common trap when one borrows a significant amount of money from the other. While unspoken, it was assumed that the one who borrowed would pay back the loan. As months turn into years, the

57 Is the Number One Relationship Killer Threatening You? (Psychology Today). Jan. 20, 2015. https://www.psychologytoday.com/us/blog/tech-support/201501/is-the-number-one-relationship-killer-threatening-you#:~:text=Research%20shows%20that%20it's%20mainly,other%20types%20of%20marital%20conflict.%E2%80%9D

lending friend grows frustrated and then angry. Eventually, a rift forms and as time marches on, their friendship dissolves.

Money is called a root of all kinds of evil, but it can do a great deal of good as well. Money is going to affect almost every aspect of your life, whether you realize it or not, whether you acknowledge that or not.

Unless you detach yourself from society and live independently in the wilderness or wilds of wherever you are in the world, completely disconnected from people, products, services, and everything else, there's really no way to avoid that simple fact.

When financial decisions align with what genuinely improves life satisfaction, money is often a **stabilizing force**.

When they do not, even strong financial systems can feel oddly empty.

THE QUIET QUESTION BEHIND EVERY FINANCIAL DECISION

There's an (often) unspoken question that lies behind every single financial choice we must make:

Will this make life *better*?

It would seem relatively obvious, wouldn't it? Wouldn't you assume that earning more money is going to make life better? Doesn't it seem reasonable to think that a bigger savings account will make you happier? Don't you think that having a larger retirement account will bring you more lasting peace as you move throughout your life?

Of course that's what most of us *assume*. We're programmed to think that way by society and its expectations. The problem lies in how life moves.

It doesn't follow human expectations or assumptions. It just… goes wherever it wants and follows whatever unexpected circumstances are thrust into its path.

The human experience doesn't often follow a simple pattern. It ebbs and flows, rises and falls, shifts and jostles like the roiling of the sea when storms roll in and when it grows completely still and calm.

Yes, research into well-being has consistently found that while financial security can certainly improve some levels of life satisfaction[58], it only goes so far.

The relationship between additional wealth and happiness grows a lot more complicated. Once you move beyond basic stability, it's not a hard and fast rule anymore.

Money helps, sure, but not always how people expect.

For far too many people, financial success –though it may feel wonderful at first— ends up leaving them feeling surprisingly empty[59].

You read that right.

Their financial life might have improved, but the person doesn't feel any different. Not really.

They spend years pursuing financial goals, they pour into them with intense focus, sacrifice time with family and friends, delay gratification, sacrifice leisure, and even though they meet some of their milestones, satisfaction doesn't seem to last long.

The stress remained. The busy schedules held firm. The sense of urgency never dissipated.

58 How Financial Security Can Impact Your Mental Well-being (Mutual of Omaha). May 15, 2024. https://www.mutualofomaha.com/advice/health-and-well-being/mental-health/how-financial-security-can-impact-your-mental-well-being

59 Why Successful People Feel Empty (Konnected Minds Podcast). Apr. 18, 2025. https://www.youtube.com/watch?v=jo_1-I6vouI&t=16s

It was not because their financial goals were wrong.

It was because money alone cannot define a fulfilling life.

WHAT ACTUALLY IMPROVES LIFE SATISFACTION

There are numerous studies that consistently point to several factors that influence life satisfaction[60]. These include:

- Meaningful relationships,
- A sense of purpose,
- Autonomy over time and decisions,
- Physical and mental health,
- Opportunities for growth and contribution.

Money intersects with all these factors, but it does not create them. Sure, a higher income is going to allow you more flexibility with many things, but if you're constantly stressed by working long hours, any real benefits might be completely wiped out.

You may also find that spending more money on experiences will have a greater positive impact on strengthening relationships, which tends to improve life satisfaction, rather than spending it on material upgrades.

Understanding these dynamics helps people use money more intentionally. But don't forget or overlook the fact that companies invest *billions* of dollars every year in marketing ***specifically*** to try and make you believe that buying their products or services will change your life for the better.

Yet, they rarely ever do.

60 Ren, Yue, et al. The Influence of Subjective Socioeconomic Status on Life Satisfaction: The Chain Mediating Rols of Social Equity and Social Trust (National Library of Medicine). Nov. 25, 2022. https://pmc.ncbi.nlm.nih.gov/articles/PMC9738263/#:~:text=Abstract,equity%20perceptions%20and%20social%20trust.

THE TIME—MONEY TRADEOFF

Have you ever heard the expression, "Time is money"?

Many of us have, but what does it mean? At its core, it means that you have to trade time for money. Or that if you're spending your time playing or goofing off or doing nothing, you're losing money because you're not earning any.

Money is currency, the ability to obtain items or services based on an agreed upon term. So, when you think about time being money, it essentially says that time is a form of currency. And it is.

You will trade time for money. We do it all the time, every day, whether we realize it or not.

Working more hours increases income, but you have less time for family or friends or other things you enjoy.

Convenience purchases cost money, but they might save time.

There's a balance you need to decide on. For yourself. No one can (or should) determine how that balance looks. That's something only you can decide for yourself.

Some people would rather maximize their income early in their careers so they can create long-term flexibility. The problem tends to be that you are likely to earn a lot less during those early years.

Other people prioritize their relationships with friends, family, or dating over working long hours.

One approach isn't 'more correct' than the other. What matters is *awareness*.

When you make these important financial decisions consciously, you are more likely to align them with your personal values and convictions rather than with cultural expectations.

Speaking of cultural expectations… modern culture tends to push one narrative: that more is *always* better.

- More income.
- More investments.
- More productivity.

This can certainly motivate people, but it also runs the risk of creating a quiet dissatisfaction among people for the present, the here and now.

When this is the expectation, then once you begin to achieve financial progress, your focus will likely shift to the next milestone.

You rarely have time to celebrate the current victory or relish the hard work you put into reaching it.

The finish line moves. And it'll move again. And again. And again.

There is a real risk of this pattern continuing indefinitely if you're not engaged in careful reflection. Life eventually becomes a series of postponed satisfactions. You'll find yourself constantly waiting for the next achievement.

It's important, then, to learn to recognize "enough." As we discussed earlier, when you can define 'enough,' it will interrupt this cycle of always needing more or the next win or the next goal.

This is what will allow for progress without permanent dissatisfaction and Aarav The Serenity Genie™ will help you in this endeavor.

SPENDING THAT SUPPORTS A GOOD LIFE

If you accept the argument that money is meant to support life satisfaction, then an important question arises:

How should we spend in ways that allow that?

Research and observation suggest that certain types of spending consistently improve well-being[61].

1. **Spending that reduces daily stress.** There are plenty of tools and resources available today that can free mental energy for more meaningful activities.
2. **Spending that strengthens relationships.** When you have positive shared experiences with someone important to you, that will tend to produce more lasting satisfaction than individual purchases.
3. **Spending that supports health and growth.** It doesn't matter whether it's in education, wellness, or even fitness, when you invest in your health and well-being, that's going to influence your present and future quality of life (as long as you stay involved in it).
4. **Spending that aligns with personal values.** When you spend money on things that matter to your values, whether it's on products or services or charities, satisfaction will generally tend to increase.

This doesn't mean every purchase you make has to serve some higher purpose. As I've talked about throughout this book, life isn't an all-or-nothing sum game. Small pleasures and comfort purchases are fine.

---

61 Kira M. Newman. How Spending Influences Happiness (Greater Good Magazine). June 6, 2016. https://greatergood.berkeley.edu/article/item/how_spending_influences_happiness#:~:text=According%20to%20a%20new%20study%20published%20in,income%20or%20total%20spending%20and%20life%20satisfaction.

The point is to understand that *some* spending will have a positive impact on quality of life so that you can **prioritize** in a way that **best fits *your* life.**

Now, one of the greatest obstacles you're going to find when it comes to life satisfaction is *comparison.*

I also mentioned this in the beginning of this book.

Modern technology allows people to see what others *want* them to see, which is usually only the *best* aspects of their life (and those videos and images and posts are often curated, edited, and polished).

These are only glimpses of life. But we are exposed to them every day, many times throughout each day, from the time we wake up to the time we close our eyes to sleep at night (if we're looking, that is).

We see vacations, homes, careers, families, and even purchases... all displayed in ways that make comparison almost unavoidable.

When this happens repeatedly, a subtle shift in your perception starts to occur. Instead of asking yourself whether your life feels satisfying, you begin to ask whether their life (the people you constantly see posting on social media) looks impressive.

Too often, this subtle shift in perspective results in spending decisions that focus on appearance rather than your genuine well-being.

We need to either break this cycle (if we've done it) or keep it from happening (if we haven't). We can do this by keeping one simple question front and center in our daily lives:

Does this (purchase, etc.) improve my life, or does it simply match someone else's?

When you ask and answer that question honestly, you'll have better clarity moving forward.

DESIGNING A FINANCIAL LIFE AROUND VALUES

What matters most to you?

For some, it's religion. For others, it's the house they live in. For others, it's helping people in need. For others, it's building a business. Still, for others, it's family. Or creativity. Or community.

You need to have a clear understanding of the values that matter most in your life.

If you don't have any clear view on what values you hold most dear, you're going to be most susceptible to the shifting sands of what society or culture says is important.

But once your priorities are clear, financial decisions become easier to evaluate. You'll find yourself asking things like:

- *Does this purchase (or expense) support what matters?*
- *Does this opportunity move life closer to what is meaningful to me?*
- *Does this item align with my values?*

The moment you have a financial system or systems that aligns with your personal values, money becomes less confusing. It becomes a tool to use rather than a confusing puzzle.

PERSONAL ACTION STEP 19: SATISFACTION

I'd like you to take some time to reflect on this question honestly:

If my financial life were working exactly the way I hoped, what would my days look like?

Some ideas to meditate on would be:

- *Would I work fewer hours?*
- *Would I spend more time with my family?*

- *Would I travel?*
- *Would I pursue creative endeavors?*
- *Would I volunteer more or contribute to causes I care about more?*

Take some time to think about this **first**, then write down whatever comes to mind.

Serenity Aligned™ (see back of book) provides ample space to enter your responses, and then, as you provide more insights, give you clarity by organizing them in order of how often you essentially say the same thing (even if it's worded differently or you didn't even think two entries were related… or simply forgot that you already wrote it down).

When you contribute to this exercise, you'll find that your attention shifts away from abstract *numbers* toward a lived experience. And lived experience is what money should ultimately support.

PREPARING FOR THE FINAL STEP

This *is* the final step: understanding the **relationship** between money and life satisfaction.

Once you have financial systems that create stability, and once your financial decisions align with what's meaningful to you, something important becomes possible:
Life stops revolving around money.
Money quietly supports the life you *want* to build.

In the final chapter, we will bring these ideas together and explore how financial peace emerges… not from perfect control, but from steady systems, realistic expectations, and a healthier relationship with money.

For now, it's enough to remember that:
Money is powerful not because of what it accumulates, but because of what it allows life to become.

CHAPTER 19

Financial Peace is Quieter Than You Think

Financial peace settles in quietly.

— — —

Brian long suffered under financial pain. Most of it was his own doing, his own failings. Growing up, he was shielded by the big income and solid wealth of his father. With a nuclear family surrounding him (father, mother, and two siblings), spending his formative years in a suburban, safe community, he wasn't exposed to many of the struggles and hardships that plague so many others.

He also hadn't been supported and encouraged properly about the things that mattered most. His father was distant, emotionally and educationally. He didn't impart wisdom for working, staying within your earnings, or delaying gratification. In fact, Brian's father tended to use purchases as replacements for love and affection.

In other words, he bought good favor with others through materialism. When Brian slipped sideways through college, doing just enough to earn a degree (paid in full by his father), he then drifted through the first years of adulthood with no direction, clarity, or economic roadmap.

He struggled. Went broke. Turned to family for help. For a long time, his father or mother or siblings 'bailed him out,' but eventually they finally realized they needed to withdrew that help and hope he figured it out.

As he moved into his forties, he began to grasp the seemingly simplest concepts of financial responsibility, but the overall picture didn't change for him. It grew into a rise and fall of small wins and big losses, lies and deceptions, and doing only just 'enough' work to get by before slipping down in debt again.

Brian listened to the experts. He read some books. He took on the typical financial tools. He worked on his debt.

When he started on those journeys (and he did that a few times), the ***picture*** of financial success at the end of the road was dramatic.

- Debt free.
- Savings in the six figures.
- Investments to make his father proud.
- Stress completely gone.

For Brian and too many others, financial peace is thought of as a big, final milestone. The finish line in a multi-year marathon.

It's viewed (usually in the beginning) as a sudden shift from struggle to security.

But as we've seen throughout this book, financial peace simply doesn't arrive that way. Often, it appears quietly, a little at a time.

THE GRADUAL CHANGE MOST PEOPLE DON'T NOTICE

I want to be very clear on this vital point:

Financial peace usually does *not* arrive through a single breakthrough.

No. It tends to grow through small shifts in your life, in your behavior, in your decisions. And these small shifts begin to accumulate over time.

Like the snowball that rolls down a steep snow-blanketed hill, gathering speed and size until it becomes a mass of size and weight large enough to blast through the seemingly impenetrable walls of debt and doubt.

Some of those small shifts might be:

- You check your accounts without anxiety.
- The unexpected expenses feel manageable rather than catastrophic.
- Financial decisions now only take a few minutes whereas they used to take hours or days of worry and fear.

Just because these changes seem small at the time don't make them insignificant. Taken together, they represent something big.

Take a dollar and go out to a bazaar, high-end market, or even with a plan to start a billion-dollar company and what would happen?

You'd probably go home with that same dollar. But surround it with more dollars and more and more until you have a large stack of cash and your story changes.

That's what it's like when you focus on these small shifts in your financial life.

Your relationship with money begins to change with every little bit of success. That shift in relationship… that's where real financial peace truly begins.

WHAT THIS BOOK HAS BEEN ABOUT

Throughout this book, we have explored several ideas that challenge common assumptions about money.

We started by pointing out that too many financial situations tend to inspire a sense of guilt and that guilt has no place in this. We talked about how simple discipline and intelligence don't have the same influence over financial decisions that circumstances, volatility, and behavioral patterns do.

We explored how scarcity changes the way people *think*, which ultimately narrows focus and increases short-term pressure.

We examined patterns, emotional spending, and financial styles, not as personal flaws, but as understandable responses to stress and uncertainty.

We also focused on building stability (and breathing room) before pursuing optimization.

All these things share a common theme and I want you to understand this key theme:

Financial progress *begins* with understanding, *not* judgment.

It is crucial that you get this: **stability comes *before* perfection.**

In fact, you're never going to attain perfection. So don't even bother trying to pursue it.

Stability is what matters. This looks like:

- Breathing room.
- Predictable systems.
- Clear priorities.

When you finally achieve stability, everything else becomes easier.

- Saving feels possible.
- Investing becomes less intimidating.
- Planning becomes realistic rather than overwhelming.

Perfection doesn't matter. Steady progress is what we need to focus on.

THE QUIET POWER OF SYSTEMS

Another theme you hopefully picked up on that runs throughout this book is the **role of systems**.

These systems can be:

- Patterns
- Automation
- Simplified structures

These carry far more weight than momentary bursts of motivation. Yeah, sure, you can feel incredibly motivated to do something, but what happens when a few days of effort don't produce the results you expected?

Motivation is emotional, but systems are structural. When systems work well, you'll need less energy to make important financial decisions. And the best choices for you and your family become easier to repeat.

A sense of calmness overtakes those who build the right systems instead of relying on motivation to carry them through.

Willpower only goes so far. Willpower is expressly dependent on energy, and as we have seen, when you're dealing with financial stress, you're expending a lot of limited energy and mental and emotional resources on that. There's nothing left over for motivation or willpower.

When you no longer have to rely on willpower to forge ahead, then your financial life becomes sustainable.

A NEW RELATIONSHIP WITH MONEY

If you've participated actively in this journey throughout the book, have you noticed any change in your relationship with money? Or how you view it?

I hope you have.

For many of us, money begins as a source of tension.

- It might feel unpredictable.
- It feels judgmental (when you make a purchase).
- It feels like something that constantly demands your attention.

As stability begins to take root and grow and expand in your life, as systems begin to take shape, money begins to change in your view.

Doesn't it become a little quieter? You're not lying awake at night, struggling to find rest. You don't have to worry as much as you did in the past.

All of that is working in the background now where it once took center stage.

When money grows quieter in your life, another important thing begins to happen: life grows louder.

The moment you start noticing your financial stress diminishing, you find there's more space for other things.

You have more time and energy for relationships, which allows them the chance to grow deeper. If you're a creative person, then you'll have more time to pursue those outlets. You have energy for hobbies that are of interest to you.

Maybe you even believe you can actually *rest* for a change, and that it will be genuinely refreshing.

These kinds of changes are not sudden most of the time. Or dramatic. They happen gradually. Softly.

It's one of the best feelings when you wake up one day and realize that money no longer dominates your every thought or decision. It now **supports** the life you are building.

LETTING GO OF THE MYTH OF "BEING BEHIND"

You've learned that believing you're 'behind' with your financial life is one of the most harmful beliefs you can hold.

- Behind your friends.
- Behind financial expectations you had x number of years ago.
- Behind some invisible timeline someone else built for you.

Life isn't a race. Nor is your financial life. People start at different places. They begin with different tools. They have different ideas and viewpoints and priorities. They face different challenges and circumstances. They encounter different obstacles as well as unique opportunities.

Comparing yourself to anyone else is a fool's errand. And it's not going to provide any useful insight.

The only beneficial comparison to make is between **who you were** and ***who you are becoming now***.

CONTINUING THE JOURNEY

The goal of this book wasn't to be a rigid blueprint. Nor was it to be a firm 'how to' in terms of where you were when you started reading it.

I never wanted you to memorize rules.

The goal is rooted in understanding that financial life changes. Income shifts. Priorities become altered. Perceptions drift. Circumstances arise and move in unexpected directions.

I want you to develop a healthier relationship with money. One that is going to allow you to respond *thoughtfully* rather than reactively.

That will allow for adaptation. And adaptability is one of the most valuable skills you can develop.

PERSONAL ACTION STEP 20: FINAL REFLECTION

It's time for a **final reflection**.

If you take away just one idea from this book, let it be this:

Financial stability is *not* built through punishment or pressure.

It's built through understanding, patience, and systems that work with human behavior rather than against it.

You don't have to change who you are to improve your financial life. You just need to have structures that support the person you *already are!*

Take a few minutes to read and re-read the highlighted statement above. Reflect on it.

Remember it. And continue to use Serenity Aligned™ (see back of book). It offers a gentle guide, encourages you to show up for yourself, and listens. (see back of book)

It will be there long after you finish the last page of this book.

LOOKING FORWARD

As we turn the page and head away from this book toward lasting peace and serenity, keep in mind this fundamental truth: progress is rarely dramatic. It usually unfolds through small increments, consistent habits, and occasional course corrections.

Some months may seem easier than others. Some of your plans will have to change.

That's okay. That's actually normal.

We're not aiming for flawless perfection. The goal is steady movement toward a life that is calmer, more stable, and more aligned with what matters most to you.

Serenity Aligned™ (see back of book) and Aarav The Serenity Genie™ were built to help you continue this journey, offering you a personal guided coach to help you move forward to the life you desire. (see back of book)

Ultimately, financial peace is not about reaching a specific number. It's about reaching a different relationship with money.

We want a relationship where:

- Decisions feel manageable
- The future feels possible
- Money supports life rather than dominating it

When you get there, peace will grow quietly, steadily, one step at a time.

For now, that's more than enough.

Here's to your new life and relationship with money...

...in peace.

Serenity Aligned ™

Is the first behavioral App that cracks the code on why you feel broke, lonely, and scared, and helps you fix it.

And then there's **Aarav The Serenity Genie™**, only availble thru the App. Your 24/7 AI personal companion who knows your pattern, remembers every step of your journey, and shows up exactly when you need him.

SerenityDecoded.com

www.ingramcontent.com/pod-product-compliance
Lightning Source LLC
LaVergne TN
LVHW021136160826
845679LV00023B/1926

* 9 7 9 8 9 9 6 0 1 0 4 0 0 *